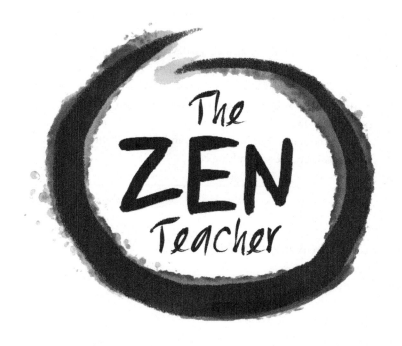

The
ZEN
Teacher

The Zen Teacher
© 2015 by Daniel Tricarico

This book is available at special discounts when purchased in quantity for use as premiums, promotions, fundraising, and educational use. For inquiries and details, contact us: shelley@daveburgessconsulting.com.

Published by Dave Burgess Consulting, Inc.
San Diego, CA
http://daveburgessconsulting.com

Cover Design by Genesis Kohler
Editing and Interior Design by My Writers' Connection

Library of Congress Control Number: 2015951195
Paperback ISBN: 978-0-9861554-6-8
Ebook ISBN: 978-0-9861554-7-5

First Printing: September 2015

To Tatum Ann and Tessa Marie

You need not leave your room.
Remain sitting at your table and listen.
You need not even listen, simply wait.
You need not even wait, just learn to be quiet
And still and solitary.
The world will freely offer itself to you
To be unmasked. It has no choice;
It will roll in ecstasy at your feet.
—*Franz Kafka*

Contents

Space, Stillness, and Self-Care

The ZEN Teacher

Introduction

The goal is the path.
—*Zen saying*

By the time I retire, I will have spent more than thirty years of my life teaching in a classroom. Furthermore, I will have spent the majority of those years in the same classroom. And when I plop down in my La-Z-Boy and toss the shawl across my knees, I will have taught nearly 6,000 students. Throw in summer school, extended assignments, serving as club advisor, and tutoring students after school, and I wouldn't be surprised if that number was double.

Working in education is different than many other jobs in that, unless one becomes an administrator, a teacher typically enters the classroom in his early twenties and leaves in his early-to-mid sixties exactly where he started. In other words, there is no corporate ladder to speak of. So in 1997, after realizing that a mortgage and a family would take more money than my teaching credentials alone could provide, I earned my master's degree in educational administration.

I realized early on, however, that the front office experience wasn't for me. It wasn't the long hours, supervising school dances, handling student referrals, monitoring behavior problems, or even dealing with the endless bureaucracy and piles of paperwork that deterred me. Rather, it would have taken me out of the classroom, and teaching is my passion. I wanted to be in a classroom with students, hovering over a text, a project, or a piece of writing, our sleeves rolled up, toiling together to create something or (if we were lucky) to make something better.

To me, that is teaching—that is the path.

In our profession, the movement is not up, but out. Our influence in the world has a ripple effect, like concentric circles on the surface of a lake. The students we encounter enter their adulthoods deeply changed by the experiences they have with us. We leave a footprint and, thanks to our students, that footprint gets passed on to the future. And while it's difficult to pay your mortgage with a metaphorical footprint, it's a pretty profound way to spend your career and to, as Steve Jobs said, "make a dent in the universe."

We all know dispassionate teachers who do it for the paycheck and for whom teaching does not even begin to approach a "calling." I feel sorry for these folks. While it's true that they are still capable of solid, competent work, I mourn the absence of passion that would make their (and by extension, their students') experience transcendent. I wish they knew the joy of the effort, the sweet exhaustion of the process, the motivating frustration of the "almost right" lesson, and the sleepy-eyed feeling of satisfaction that comes from knowing you're on an important, meaningful journey—even if they are, like me, driving a 1998 Buick Century that has bald tires, a digital odometer that died six months after purchasing the car, and a steering wheel that is crumbling to pieces in their hands. And even though I am sometimes embarrassed to rattle up to the corner grocery store, I know there is a nobility to my pursuits.

As teachers, we are given an amazing opportunity to influence young people and profoundly affect how they see the world. It's an awe-inspiring privilege, but it's also a challenge. In the last decade, I've seen a number of excellent teachers break down, crash and burn, or just plain leave the profession. This is a result of the stressors they've encountered at their schools or in their classrooms and also because the industry has, in many ways, gone plain "loco." My school has also witnessed a significant drop in the number of student-teacher applicants, a sobering indication that fewer people view teaching as a viable career. It's a shame.

That's why I began The Zen Teacher blog and eventually wrote this book. I am devoted to showing teachers how to maintain a sense of focus, simplicity, and tranquility in the face of the obstacles and problems the modern American educator encounters daily. I want to show them that they can not just survive, but thrive in the classroom.

Teachers do incredibly important and influential work—and they do it almost entirely devoid of the concrete, culturally valued rewards associated with professional employment, such as the big paycheck, the luxury car, or the corner office with the stunning view. Despite the limited tangible rewards, there is, perhaps, no career as fulfilling to the soul as education. This noble profession can provide a deep sense of Zen tranquility because we know that the ripples we create today can influence and even improve tomorrow. The path we travel day in and day out with our students—and the manner in which we travel—is important. And if the goal is the path, then it helps to love the path.

What is Zen?

The white cloud is always the white cloud. The blue mountain is always the blue mountain.
—*Tozan, Zen Master*

The warmth of the sun. The greenness of the grass. The cries of a child.

When you notice your world exactly as it is—free from judgment and with detachment from anticipated outcomes—that is Zen.

Finding a moment of Zen can be a profoundly deep and meaningful pursuit. In that moment, you are fully present and are experiencing life in a way that the rest of the world—in its insane marathon of haste, chaos, and busyness—typically ignores.

Tuned into the actuality of the present moment, you are living life.

As it happens.

Right now.

The pursuit of a Zen moment can begin with a practice as simple as focusing on your breathing, which is the life force that ties you to both the earth and to your soul, your essence, your inner being.

So take a moment.

Get in touch with the natural rhythm of your breath.

Breathe in. Breathe out.

Look around. Notice your surroundings.

Do not judge.

Just experience.

Sense what you sense.

Experience a Zen moment.

Throughout this book, you will find concepts, activities, and techniques that teach you how to incorporate Zen practices in a way that will not only transform your teaching style but also your life. With practice, they will leave you feeling more centered, focused, and peaceful.

In some ways, Zen is a very simple concept that is immediately understood. In other ways, however, this "simple" skill can take a lifetime to master.

And if that's the case, then we'd better get started.

Zen Practice

The archer ceases to be conscious of himself as the one
who is engaged in hitting the bull's-eye which confronts
him. This state of unconsciousness is realized only when,
completely empty and rid of the self, he becomes one
with the perfecting of his technical skill, though there is
in it something of a quite different order which cannot
be attained by any progressive study of the art.
—*Eugene Herrigel, Zen in the Art of Archery*

Everything **I ever needed to know about Zen,** I learned from
Disneyland. If my family was planning a trip to the Magic
Kingdom, the weeks before were pure torture. I spent all my waking hours waiting in agony. Waiting for my parents to tell us what time
we were leaving. Waiting for school to end. Waiting to pack up the car in
the morning, my eyes heavy with sleep, my heart pounding with antici-
pation. I focused most of my brainpower on our upcoming trip—picking
the first ride I wanted to go on and thinking about which restaurants
had the best food. I engaged in deep, philosophical discussions with my
friends about the relative value of Tomorrowland versus Fantasyland.

And sleep the night before? Forget it!

The next thing I knew, I was waking up the morning after the trip,
with only one question floating through my mind: What in the world
just happened?

I had dreamed, for so long, of going on the Matterhorn, Haunted Mansion, and Pirates of the Caribbean rides, and now, suddenly, the trip was over. All I had were memories. What happened, I wondered, to the actual trip itself? Why did I have no recollection of actually being at Disneyland, no sense of enjoying the music, watching the parades, riding the rides, or snacking on popcorn and soda?

Why was it already over?

The answer, of course, is because—at the time—I had been totally immersed in the moment.

Even as a child standing in line for the Jungle Cruise, my Present Moment Awareness (more about that later) was so amplified and my inability to appreciate my immediate experience so pronounced that the actual adventure came and went without my having a real conscious sense of actually having had it. The irony was that I was intuitive enough to be in the moment, but I wasn't quite enlightened enough to know how to acknowledge or appreciate the moment I was in, and so it slipped by me, completely unnoticed and unacknowledged.

I was focused. I was experiencing.

I was so there that the next thing I knew, I wasn't.

That's Zen for you. My youthful trips to Disneyland, therefore, can be counted as one of my earliest experiences with a Zen Practice.

To purists, "Zen Practice" typically refers to *zazen*, a sitting meditation that teaches participants how to completely immerse themselves into the present moment. While initially a facet of Zen Buddhism, Zen, when used as a philosophy, is not connected to any particular religion or doctrine and can be practiced by someone of any faith or religious persuasion. For our somewhat broader purpose, I'd like to suggest that your Zen Practice can be any activity that helps you hone your focus, improve your ability to stay rooted in the present, and be fully aware of what is happening directly before you.

Zen is similar to what university professor Mihaly Csikszentmihalyi named "Flow"—a state of being in which you are so totally engaged by an experience that everything else melts away and you lose track of time.

Zen, when used as a philosophy, is not connected to any particular religion.

It's what athletes and artists describe when they say they're "in the zone." If you were to call a friend and she said, "I'm sorry; I was outside gardening, and I lost track of time. I almost didn't hear the phone ring," she was participating in her own Zen Practice.

This is, in part, what German philosopher Eugen Herrigel was referring to in the quote at the start of this chapter when he said, "The archer ceases to be conscious of himself." And though Herrigel said part of a Zen Practice is the pursuit of the technical skill, he also suggested there is "something of quite a different order which cannot be obtained" by practicing—that is, the spiritual side. A Zen Practice allows you to lose yourself to a greater sense of intuition, intensity, and energy that arises from both the focus on, and the detachment from, the activity at hand.

For me, surfing always seemed to be one of the most quintessential Zen Practices. A single person (the surfer) makes attempt after attempt to become one with an element of nature (the wave) and experiences both Yin (riding the wave) and Yang (frequent and inglorious wipeouts). The amateur surfer receives no money or other compensation for his efforts. There is no finish line, no winners, and no losers. So why do it? Because the surfer has found something that allows him to practice peace, experience flow, and become one with nature.

Teaching, too, can be a Zen Practice. When you are in your classroom, completely focused on your students or captivated by the lesson you're presenting, that's Zen. Perhaps you were caught up in your lecture on the Trail of Tears, or lost in the physics project where students built and operated a balloon launcher, or maybe you were moved by a scene in the drama class where the student actors were totally present and in touch with the reality of the moment. Teaching's ability to help us stay in the moment is one of our profession's greatest gifts and why it shares such a kinship with Zen. When our teaching comes from who we are and originates from our passions and our heart, we increase the likelihood that we will experience flow and be "in the zone." Being open to what may happen, without sticking to rigid, anticipated outcomes, and showing compassion and gratitude to those you encounter in the classrooms, the hallways, and the administration office allows you to treat your teaching moments as potentially transcendent experiences.

In the interest of balance, you may also want to develop a Zen Practice outside the classroom. It can be any hobby or activity, as long as it provides an experience that takes you beyond the immediate con-

> *You can intentionally create your own Zen moments in the classroom, which can lead to a great sense of peace and centeredness.*

straints of time and space and that replenishes your energy, passion, and vitality as a teacher. For some, as I said, it might be surfing. For you, it may be writing, sewing, singing, painting, acting, running, hiking, or bicycling. The key is to find a pursuit that is in sync with your personal rhythms and for which you can muster a bit of passion so that the practice will be fun and effortless.

My father used music to pursue his own sense of Zen, though he never would have called it that. In the evenings, after putting in a full day's work at his day job and then toiling a few more hours at a second job, my father sat in his recliner, turned on some classic rock or the blues, put his head back, and he was gone. He would mentally detach and remove himself from the worries of the day. Having witnessed these musical odysseys growing up, I have no doubt that he was truly "in the zone." And if you ever asked him, I'm sure he'd say it was a pretty wonderful feeling.

Much in the way my father used music, as a teacher, you can intentionally create your own Zen moments in the classroom, which can lead to a great sense of peace and centeredness. With some luck and practice, you will notice a positive difference in your students as well, all as a result of you deciding to be more present and intentional with the moments you're given in the classroom.

What Is Your Zen Practice?

In *Writing Down the Bones: Freeing the Writer Within*, author Natalie Goldberg's Zen teacher asks her, "Why don't you make writing your practice? If you go deep enough in writing, it will take you every place." Like Goldberg, I think of writing as part of my Zen Practice. When a writing session is going well, there is nothing else on my radar; I am fully consumed by the words in front of me. It's a very pure, very liberating feeling, and it's one of the places in my life where I can lose myself fully in the now and truly be present.

To discover your own Zen Practice, ask yourself, "What do I love?" and "Where do I feel most in tune with the world, the universe, or myself?" This may be where you discover the essence of the activity you want to pursue. As a teacher, your answer may, of course, lie in the classroom, but what about outside of school? For example, your Zen Practice could be gardening, fishing, cooking, or anything else that lets you focus on your passions, explore your obsessions, be in the moment, and experience flow.

Where do you feel most in tune with the world, the universe, or yourself?

Remember, when you're pursuing your Zen Practice, there is no goal. There is no finish line. It's the doing—the routines, rituals, and techniques—that rewards you; the performance of the task is your prize. I know this is a wildly foreign concept because we are accustomed to wanting to know "What's in it for me?" and, even as teachers, we have a tendency to focus on achieving objectives and outcomes.

Now think back to the surfer. While the surfer can enter competitions and vie for prizes, fame, money, and adulation from adoring fans, most people who don wetsuits and paddle out onto the waves are, I suspect, just hoping to dance with the ocean one more time, feel that connection to nature or, in a less poetic sense, simply get a little exercise. They use each wave as an opportunity to improve, to maybe spend a little more time on the board before falling off.

A personal Zen Practice can be a transformative way to pursue a greater sense of fulfillment, peace, and tranquility. What's nice is that you get to decide how committed you want to be to your Zen Practice. Regardless of where you are on the path—whether you're being introduced to Zen for the first time here or are choosing to study more in a discipline you've dabbled in—I hope this book will be a stepping stone on your Zen journey.

ZEN TEACHER ASSIGNMENT

Answer these questions:

1. What do you love to do?
2. What activities do you participate in when you often lose track of time?
3. What if you engaged in them regularly and used them as vehicles for peace and focus?

If that works for you, you may have just discovered your personal Zen Practice.

Beginner's Mind

In the beginner's mind there are many
possibilities; in the expert's mind
there are few.
— *Shunryu Suzuki*

When **I was much younger,** I was always embarrassed to say, "I don't know." I felt ashamed because I saw my ignorance as a deficiency, a weakness. And yet, I knew I didn't know, and I didn't want to misrepresent my position, so I said nothing. In retrospect, I realize that admitting I had something to learn is one of the most mature and enlightened stances I could have taken.

"Beginner's Mind" refers to the practice of approaching a situation with an open mind, a vulnerable heart, and a willingness to learn. It invites curiosity, is detached from a particular or anticipated outcome, and engenders a humility deep enough to foster learning. When we approach life with Beginner's Mind, we learn to be strong enough to say, "I don't know," "I'm not sure," and, "I can learn more."

Many people I grew up with—especially those involved in organized religion—always seemed to have it all figured out, and they acted as if there was nothing left for them to learn about their beliefs. They spent our conversations espousing their opinions, white-knuckling their pre-conceived notions, and insisting on the "rightness" of their position.

With Beginner's Mind, we learn to be strong enough to say, "I don't know," "I'm not sure," and, "I can learn more."

Not only did I envy these people, I was in awe of them. They seemed content in their knowledge and secure in their position. I desperately wanted to share their confidence because finding answers has been a guiding principle of my life, and I, too, wanted to *know*.

But as I matured, my philosophy matured with me. I realized that *not* knowing or, at the very least, approaching every situation without assuming I already had all the answers typically resulted in not only a *greater* learning but also a *deeper* one. I began to look differently at the people who I thought had it all figured out. They suddenly seemed stagnant and rigid. And when they were forced to learn something or change their position on a long-held and cherished belief, they experienced a personal crisis, which caused them visible stress. Eventually, I decided I would rather *not* know everything and be surprised by the things that I learned about life.

We often become so accustomed to our rituals and ceremonies that our stagnation becomes habitualized, and then, if we aren't careful, we feel as if we are done learning. I remember saying the Lord's Prayer for the umpteenth time when I stopped one day and asked myself, "What am I really saying?" I had recited that prayer since I was a child, but not once could I recall bothering to question its meaning.

With a Beginner's Mind, I stopped and broke it down, line by line, and tried to make sense of it, to learn what it actually meant. Not only did my understanding of the prayer deepen, but my overall spirituality did as well.

Consider the rote way the Pledge of Allegiance is said in schools. What if teachers and students stopped and asked themselves, "What am I really saying?" or "What does 'indivisible' actually mean, anyway?" How could Beginner's Mind help us better understand this statement of unity?

As educators, the people who are supposed to have all the answers, adopting Beginner's Mind can have powerful implications. I was once tutoring a student for the SAT, for example, when we encountered a small conflict. The SAT required a twenty-five-minute timed writing essay, and my student insisted on only using one piece of supporting evidence per paragraph. I told him the expectation was two, and his score would be higher if he used multiple examples. As the tutor, *the learned one*, I was indignant that this young upstart thought he knew more about writing and standardized testing than me, a seasoned veteran with both private tutoring and classroom experience.

The following week, however, I checked with my school's Advanced Placement English teacher (who also taught SAT prep classes). She said that the College Board's position was that one piece of supporting evidence per paragraph was enough if it was properly developed.

At our next session, I explained to my student that he was right. I learned something new, which never would have happened had I stuck to my position as the "expert" who knew everything and had nothing left to learn.

In the classroom, the Beginner's Mind philosophy allows you to embrace an open-mindedness and vulnerability that will improve both the quality and, more importantly, the *depth* of learning that occurs, for both you and your students. It can influence the way you design and implement your lessons and free you to admit that you are not the

Adopting the liberating stance of "not knowing" opens a myriad of possibilities.

Gatekeeper of All Knowledge. This freedom enables both you and your students to enjoy the adventure of exploration and discovery that comes with learning. Adopting the liberating stance of "not knowing" opens a myriad of possibilities. Openness combined with curiosity allows us to see more clearly, hear more accurately, understand more fully, and risk more freely. Unrestricted by what we think we know, we are more inclined to try and less inclined to judge ourselves so harshly when we fail.

ZEN TEACHER ASSIGNMENT

Think of the last time you learned something new and then reflect on the following questions:

How did you approach that situation?

What was your perspective?

What were you thinking?

How did your outlook in those circumstances differ from times when you felt like you knew what you were doing and had already garnered some experience?

What would the benefits be if you entered into every situation as if you were a novice, as if you had something to learn?

What then?

The Living Dead

The unpardonable sin is the sin of
inadvertence, of not being alert,
not quite awake.
—*Joseph Campbell*

These days it's hip to be prepared for the zombie apocalypse.
But sometimes it feels like the apocalypse has already happened.
So many of us spend our days powering through life, racing from
one thing to another, unable (or unwilling) to slow down, uninterested in
waking up and seeing what is right in front of us. As a result, we often lurch
through our lives like extras in George A. Romero's *Night of the Living Dead*.

If you haven't noticed these modern-day zombies, you may be one.
I know I certainly can be. On any given day, you'll often find me staring
into the eerie glow of my phone or tablet, glued to the Internet, or otherwise buried in my work.

As author Joseph Campbell said, "The unpardonable sin is the sin
of inadvertence, of not being alert, not quite awake." Calling inadvertence, the act of not paying attention, an unpardonable sin is a strong
statement, but he's right. To be a zombie in this world is to waste the gift
we've been given, to disrespect and devalue our lives, and to neglect the

beauty surrounding us in favor of behaving like a machine. Unaddressed, our own inadvertence can kill our spirits and deaden our hearts.

Experiencing life involves being deliberate with our attention, mindful of our choices, and intentional with our focus.

So what does it mean to be awake?

It means slowing down, being alert to our environment, and not getting stuck in the mind/heart drain of modern society's hyper-paced vortex. Waking up means wanting less stuff, tolerating less noise, and engaging in fewer obligations so that you can take a breath without taking on a new responsibility or carrying around baggage from the past. It's about being present and fully experiencing your surroundings, whether that means pausing to really look at your loved ones, listening to your child's story, feeling your dog's fur between your fingers as you pet him, or noticing the colors of the sunset. It means noticing the red barn in the middle of the emerald meadow, smelling the soft rain, tasting the purple onion on the barbecued hamburger, or listening to "Hey Jude" by Wilson Pickett, solely to appreciate Duane Allman's guitar solo.

Waking up means noticing, observing, feeling, watching, caring, breathing, and enjoying. Waking up means being present. Every day.

Experiencing life involves being deliberate with our attention, mindful of our choices, and intentional with our focus. Creative people—painters, actors, poets, dancers—intuitively understand this idea of awareness. Their pursuits are inherently mindful and require them to stop, capture individual moments, and celebrate the immediate. We can learn from their approach and apply it to our classrooms.

To make the most of the finite moments you're allotted for your classroom, you must choose how you will spend each one. Being awake in the classroom offers particularly special rewards. When you're fully present, you'll be aware of the student who is struggling, academically or personally. You'll make the time to listen to him to see if you can help fix the problem. You'll discover new jewels in your lesson, even if you taught the concept a million times. And you'll notice changes that need to be made, whether it's the books from which you teach, the way the desks are arranged, or the lessons you design.

The best part of teaching—in fact, my favorite part—is that if you pay attention, you'll see the light turn on in a child's mind; you'll recognize the improvement, and you'll experience the joy, wonder, and magic of learning. And what in this whole world could be better than that? If you miss that moment, why even be there?

Trust me—there's no room for zombies in education.

Zen Teacher Assignment

Carve out time in your day to completely unplug from every device, every piece of technology—focus on nothing else but nature, perhaps, and the rhythm of your own breathing.

Intuition

It is by logic that we prove,
but by intuition that we discover.
—*Henri Poincaré*

It's late. Broken streetlights flicker sporadically. You're walking down the street by yourself and you notice someone coming the other way. He could be on his way home or simply looking for an open convenience store to buy milk for his toddler. But the bottom line is you're alone. Something doesn't feel right. He's done nothing to indicate he's a menace, but your stomach is sending signals to your brain, alerting you that something is off. You cross the street. And it's not until he's out of sight that you allow yourself to breathe a sigh of relief.

A stranger. A bad feeling.

The sense you should avoid contact.

This is intuition.

Sometimes intuition is called an "inner voice," "reading between the lines," "deduction," or simply "paying attention." But at a very basic level, intuition is knowing without any conscious sense of signals, details, or rationale about why you know. Intuition is the impulse responsible when a father reaches out right before his baby takes a tumble onto a sidewalk. Having been in that position, I guarantee you he will not be able to articulate exactly why he reached out at that particular moment; he just knew he should.

These subconscious signals were once called *women's* intuition because some assumed that men could not and *would not* access (and certainly would never *rely on*) their subconscious or emotions for clues on how to live. If a man even came close to trusting his intuition, he would say it was a "gut reaction." But we've all, men and women, been in a situation where we have acted based on a hunch or a feeling.

Even the military is getting into the act. The U.S. Navy started a program to study how troops use intuition in battle to gauge danger and anticipate problems. The idea for the program came from anecdotal evidence from troops who reported feeling a strange sense of danger just before encountering an attack or an explosive device. In these cases, it's not an exaggeration to say that intuition saves lives.

Based on the knowledge we've learned and experiences we've had over the years, intuition informs our judgment and our ability to make fast decisions. It's different from thinking, though, and not quite as "out there" as previously thought. As it turns out, we actually are receiving data when we have a gut feeling—we're just receiving it on a more subconscious level. As noted scientist Jonas Salk put it, "Intuition will tell the thinking mind where to look next."

Intuition informs our judgment and our ability to make fast decisions.

Artists have also long understood this. In fact, famed film director and *Twin Peaks* creator David Lynch said, "Intuition is the key to everything, in painting, filmmaking, business—everything. I think you could have an intellectual ability, but if you can sharpen your intuition, which

The more you practice and hone your intuition, the easier it becomes to notice, trust, and follow those impulses.

they say is emotion and intellect joining together, then a knowingness occurs."

So the question becomes: What does your "knowingness" look like? Can you recognize it when it happens? Can you use it to your advantage, to guide your life and help you make better decisions? I think so. It turns out that intuition is a muscle, and it can be developed, not unlike the way that you would work your pecs or glutes in the gym. Interestingly, the more you practice and hone your intuition, as Zen Teachers should, the easier it becomes to notice, trust, and follow those impulses. But tuning into intuition takes effort and practice.

How do you practice intuition? I suggest starting off by being still and quiet, which enhances your ability to listen to your inner voice. Stopping the white noise of the world allows you to burn through the day's distractions and chaos and access the deeper parts of your psyche and soul, where you can focus on the hunches that are trying to speak to you. It's more difficult to recognize intuition when you're doing a million things at once. It's harder to listen to your gut when car horns are honking, the dog is barking, and the baby's crying.

Once you're still, silent, and listening, you may recognize a twinge or a "gut feeling." At that point, stop and ask yourself, "What is this sensation alerting me to?" It may be that your subconscious has registered something, however peripherally, that needs your attention. You are then free to tune into that signal or wavelength and act on it accordingly, whether it's at home with family, say, or even in the classroom with your students.

As a committed educator, you probably already rely on intuition as a tool for excellent teaching. Have you ever anticipated when a child, who is struggling with a concept, needs a touch on the shoulder or a supportive ear? Sometimes the signs are overt, but sometimes the nuance of human behavior makes them less obvious and yet, somehow as teachers, we know—we can sense. With just a slight vibe (and often very little conscious data), we can confidently say, "This child needs help. I need to keep this student on my radar."

As Zen Teachers, we need to remember that intuition is a gift we already have—a gift we must first acknowledge, then hone, then trust.

Zen Teacher Assignment

Set aside time today to experience stillness, silence, and just tune into your intuition.

What is your gut telling you?

What vibes or signals are you receiving?

In terms of faith, where might God be leading you?

Regarding your classroom, which student needs your direction or encouragement?

What is your intuition saying to you?

Listen closely.

Non-Judgment

> To set up what you like against what you
> dislike—this is the disease of the mind.
> —Seng-Tsan

Shakespeare's tragic hero, Hamlet, said, "There is nothing either good or bad, but thinking makes it so." That philosophy still applies to life, as well as to our classrooms today. The struggles we face often come down to one thing: the difference between the way things are and the way we think they should be.

Our culture conditions us to pursue the duality of "This is great/ this is awful," all but forcing us to choose a side. But you can eliminate a truckload of dissatisfaction by adopting the more inclusive idea of saying simply, "This is." And then when "this" changes, you can say, "Now this is," and accept whatever comes your way.

Practicing non-judgment doesn't mean you can't have preferences—you can still hate chocolate ice cream, and you can still love monster truck rallies! And it doesn't mean that you don't care or that you stop striving for excellence. But when you approach situations free of judgment, you are better able to step back and see them for the temporary, ephemeral things they are.

Life will never be free of problems. As much as we might like to, we cannot change other people's behavior. But what we *can* change is how we react. Practicing the Zen tenet of non-judgment helps us control our reactions. By refusing to make judgments, we can endure challenges more effectively, and, more importantly, we can learn to persevere. When we resist the temptation to assign judgment, we aren't tossed around like sailboats in choppy waters. Instead, we will be better able to navigate life's inevitable challenges from a place of grace, equilibrium, and buoyancy.

As Zen Teachers, one of the most critical environments where we can practice non-judgment is the classroom. Imagine the increased sense of peace we would feel if, for example, we simply learned to appreciate and deal with the resources, students, and administration we have—rather than obsessing over what we think we should have. What if we did as spiritual teacher and author Ram Dass suggests when he said: "Let's trade in all our judging for appreciating. Let's lay down all our righteousness and just be together"?

> *Practicing the Zen tenet of non-judgment helps us control our reactions.*

Think about it. What would happen to your sense of peace and love if non-judgment were your default position? If you refrained from judging that knucklehead student who is the bane of your existence, how might you see him differently? Likely, you'd see him as a child who needs guidance and compassion.

Just imagine how far you could go if you decided you could learn and thrive in any circumstance! That might seem a little too *kumbaya* for some people's tastes, but then that's just them judging our behavior, isn't it? And we've just learned how futile that is!

Here are a few steps to help you reach a place of non-judgment:

1. ***Notice when you are judging something.*** Don't worry about changing your behavior. Just observe your life and notice the times when you pass judgment. The first step is merely becoming aware of your thoughts and choices.

2. ***Learn more about the situation.*** Instead of saying, "I know what that's like, and I hate it," or, "I know what that person's like and I can't stand him," try to learn more about that thing, situation, or person before dropping that hammer of judgment. A thirst for information makes it easier to choose non-judgment because you will seek to really understand what's happening. That understanding, in turn, increases your sense of empathy and compassion, which makes it much easier to ignore your impulse to judge.

3. ***Think of alternatives.*** When you are ready to change your behavior, discover other ways you can respond. Can you ignore the situation? Accept it? Laugh at it? Remove it or sidestep it? Try to develop a series of alternative responses to keep in your spiritual toolbox. When circumstances stimulate your impulse to judge, pause for a moment, dig through your toolbox, and choose a healthier, more positive reaction.

4. ***Forgive yourself.*** We're either hardwired to judge situations, people, and things, or society has trained us to do so. Either way, learning to embrace non-judgment runs counter to our conditioning. So don't expect changes overnight. When you stumble and fall into the judgment trap, accept it and forgive yourself.

Let me put it this way: You can choose to flip off and swear at the guy who cuts you off on the freeway. Or you can choose to ignore the situation, not judge the other driver, and invest the energy you saved by not raising that distinctive digit into brainstorming a more effective lesson to teach later that day. You'll feel calmer and more in control, and your students will benefit as a result.

ZEN TEACHER ASSIGNMENT

As hard as it seems, spend at least half an hour today telling yourself that, no matter what happens, you will refrain from anticipating outcomes and passing judgment. Remind yourself to let the world unfold as it pleases and glide through its ups and downs without casting judgment.

Lovingkindness

My religion is very simple.
My religion is kindness.
—*Dalai Lama*

The world can be a difficult place. If you look, you can find infinite justifications for anger, bitterness, and resentment. And you can live there, if you want, basking in the muck and the dreck, wallowing in the pain and the emotional sewage. At the same time, every moment holds innumerable opportunities to experience joy, to practice peace and love, and to cultivate an attitude of kindness. The approach we choose and where we decide to spend our time and energy make all the difference in our mental well-being and the openness and generosity of our hearts, both as educators and as citizens of the planet. *New York Times* best-selling author and meditation teacher Sharon Salzberg said, "The difference between misery and happiness depends on what we do with our attention."

That's where lovingkindness comes in.

"Lovingkindness" means approaching the world with a sense of tenderness, compassion, love, and gentility that increases our inner peace and serenity. It's an attitude that sends out positive vibrations—or signals—that calm and encourage those around us. And it can be the sword with which we defend ourselves against moments of anger and resentment, by meeting them head-on with, as the word suggests, both love and kindness.

Lovingkindness is particularly important when interacting with students, especially when we least feel like it.

The term dates back to 1535, when Myles Coverdale coined it in the Coverdale Bible, the first English translation of the entire Bible. However, no single spiritual approach has a monopoly on treating others well. The expression has found a home in a number of other religions and philosophies, including Judaism and Buddhism.

It may seem obvious, but lovingkindness is particularly important when interacting with students, especially when we least feel like it. Qualities of giving, service, compassion, kindness, and love are easy to practice during times of relative calm, when our impulse is to join hands and warble, "We Are the World." But in today's educational climate, it's easy to feel frustrated, angry, or unhappy—emotions that make it tough to show compassion and love.

If you're like me, the reticent, snarky girl in fifth period drives you nuts, and the hyperactive boy in the Red Robin reading group tests your patience. Then, just as you near your wit's end, you notice that the boy comes to class with ragged clothes, and you discover that the girl can't sleep at night because of the yelling and screaming in her home. If you keep in mind their stories and struggles, you may find it easier to offer a bit of kindness to those who least expect it.

Sometimes it seems as though teachers must be in constant loving-kindness mode. Last week, for example, I consoled a sobbing student in the office because her father had just passed away that morning. I raided my file cabinet for pretzels, Corn Nuts, and a Cup-a-Soup for another girl who came to school with no food. I responded to an email from another girl in my last class, who was absent because she had been told over the weekend that her parents were getting divorced. She said the news "broke" her, she "couldn't take it anymore," she "no longer felt needed or loved," and that "nothing would fix it." And that was just Monday and Tuesday! With all the chaos our children are forced to deal with, it's a marvel, sometimes, that any of them care at all about *The Catcher in the Rye* or quadratic equations.

Lovingkindness is essential for navigating our bell-to-bell lives. It can determine your level of happiness throughout your personal life as well. By approaching the world with a sense of lovingkindness in your classroom, home, and life, you will more fully see the connection between all things. You will also be able to more easily accept others' limits and faults (and forgive them), as well as fill your own heart with an abundance of love and peace.

You need lovingkindness *the most* when you feel overwhelmed with the business of teaching and the insanity of the profession starts to wear on you. When the education machine lays one more responsibility on you, makes another decision that is nonsensical, or, worse, damaging to you, your colleagues, or your students, it is time to reach out, to serve others, to give.

Approaching the world with compassion and kindness can ignite a sense of happiness and well-being within you. It's a Zen Teacher practice that can help you not only endure and survive those moments of insanity, but also thrive and create a better world.

> Approaching the world with compassion and kindness can ignite a sense of happiness and well-being within you.

ZEN TEACHER ASSIGNMENT

Be kind.

Compassion

Blessed are the merciful; for they shall obtain mercy.
—*Matthew 5:7 (KJV)*

You never really understand a person until you consider things from his point of view . . . until you climb into his skin and walk around in it.
—*Atticus Finch, To Kill A Mockingbird*

The Dalai Lama says in *The Art of Happiness,* "If you want others to be happy, practice compassion. If you want to be happy, practice compassion." And it's true; when we come to another person's aid, we often feel better ourselves, knowing that we helped. Some irony, huh?

As teachers, we have ample opportunity to show compassion in every hour of every class of every day. More than that, we have a special, even sacred, obligation to express compassion. Not only do we enlighten, but we are also expected to uplift those around us and to ease their struggles. In fact, showing grace and kindness to those around us can be one of our profession's greatest rewards.

When seeking to express compassion, ask, "Who is in need?" and, "How can I help?" Your answer could be the student who has attempted the math problem twenty times and still can't get it, the administrator having trouble finding a chaperone for the prom, or the first-year teacher in need of wisdom as he struggles to manage an unruly class.

Teachers meet countless people every day who could use a little dose of compassion.

Teachers meet countless people every day who could use a little dose of compassion, but, ultimately, there are three core groups who need compassion most: your students, your colleagues, and yourself.

YOUR STUDENTS

Sometimes you don't need to look for opportunities to show compassion for your students—sometimes, they find you.

I once had a student named Nick who had a severe case of social anxiety. Nick's anxiety was so pronounced that he could not function as a student in my class or even sit in the room with the other students. He would pace, whimper, and sometimes tear up because of his inability to focus. When I asked him where his anxiety was coming from (me? his home life? his peers?), he would just pace, his hands pressed against his temples, and say, "I don't know. I don't know. I don't know."

He often showed up in my classroom during lunch where we would eat and talk until class started. As soon as the bell rang and other students began to file into the room, Nick excused himself to my office. After starting the other students on their work, I made my way back into the office to get Nick going on the same assignment.

To help with his condition, Nick was eventually transferred out of my class and put in a program more suitable to his needs. As is often the case in education, I was never told how he finally made out, but I hope that whatever compassion I showed him helped ease at least some of his discomfort. But here's the thing: If I hadn't expressed compassion for Nick's situation, nobody would have benefited. If I had merely ignored his discomfort and anxiety, the situation may have been even more uncomfortable for Nick, me, and the rest of his classmates, who,

I say with great pride in their character, recognized Nick's situation and were extraordinarily compassionate toward him as well.

What are your students' needs? How can you help?

YOUR COLLEAGUES

We all know colleagues who are going through difficult times, either professionally or personally. During these challenging times, offering peers your sincere and genuine compassion can be helpful. You could send a supportive email, leave encouraging notes on their desks or in their mailboxes, or maybe even lend a listening and confidential ear. Simple acts of compassion toward peers and colleagues can help cement the bond you feel with those around you and increase the sense of unity on campus.

Try asking yourself, "Who among my co-workers needs encouragement? And how can I help?"

YOURSELF

The sad truth is that we are often harsher, more critical, and more damaging to our own hearts and minds than anyone else could ever be. We ruin our health and happiness by wallowing in worry, anger, and bitterness. In the name of achievement or work ethic, we push ourselves beyond reasonable limits. Therefore, showing compassion to ourselves is necessary before we can ever offer support or empathy to anyone else.

Not too long ago, I saw an inspirational poster that said, "I was looking for someone to inspire me, motivate me, and keep me focused . . . someone who would love me, cherish me, and make me happy, and I realized that all along I was looking for myself." Self-compassion is an undervalued, under-practiced art that includes everything from forgiving yourself for perceived or actual mistakes to practicing positive self-talk, such as affirmations, praise, pleasant thoughts, and well wishes.

Compassion is both a skill and a quality, something that exists inside of us, but also something we can practice and hone. Joan Halifax, PhD, founder and head teacher of the Upaya Institute and Zen Center in Santa Fe, New Mexico, describes compassion as "the capacity to be attentive to the experience of others, to wish the best for others, and to sense what will truly serve others." And if, in our heart of hearts, we wish to develop a genuine sense of compassion because we truly care about others, we will, as Halifax suggests, be intentional about noticing and responding to what our students, our colleagues, and what we ourselves need.

ZEN TEACHER ASSIGNMENT

When learning to express compassion, don't try to save the entire world all at once. Look for a single opportunity in your classroom to express concern and empathy for an individual student—the child who is being bullied, who feels alone, who has a troubled home life, who is struggling with an academic concept, or who is hungry. Help the person next to you. Reach out and ease a single student's burden. Then go from there.

Gratitude

You have to be grateful whenever you get to
someplace safe and okay, even if it turns out it
wasn't quite where you were heading.
—*Anne Lamott, Small Victories*

B ecause I was a drama major and writer, my favorite teacher of
all time should probably have been an acting or English instruc-
tor, but he wasn't. Hands down, my favorite teacher of all time
was my high school Spanish teacher, Mr. Morrissey. He was not only
intelligent and knowledgeable in his subject area, but was wise in the way
that only the truly compassionate, intuitive, and caring can be. I learned
as much about how to be a decent person from him as I did about how
to conjugate the verb *hablar*. I realized a few years into my own teaching
career that unless students tell the teacher what the class meant to them,
the teacher may never know the impact he or she has had on a student.
So a few years later, when Mr. Morrissey was retiring, I wrote him a
letter telling him how much his compassion and wisdom meant to me
and how grateful I was to have had him as a teacher. In education, there
are an infinite number of ways, in our roles as both teacher and student,
to express a sense of gratitude. And each of those infinite ways is a gift.

When our mind is focused on what we're grateful for, it's nearly impossible to feel unhappy.

In truth, gratitude is one of the most powerful tools we have to stay grounded and to keep our spirits centered. And if we practice it regularly, gratitude reminds us of the blessings in our lives and keeps us from worrying about some slight in the past or some potential catastrophe in the future. When our mind is focused on what we're grateful for, it's nearly impossible to feel unhappy.

Maybe you're grateful to the parent who donated supplies, the staff member who obtained for you the books you needed, or the colleague who spent her prep period listening to your sob story about the morning's finger-painting disaster. The key is to seize the opportunities to acknowledge and express your own sense of appreciation.

The first step is asking yourself, "Whom can I thank?" You may find your answer during a two-minute gratitude session, a method that Leo Babauta, a best-selling author and creator of the *Zen Habits* blog, practices regularly. During these sessions, he sits quietly, focuses his mind, tunes out distractions, and spends two minutes reflecting on whom and what he's thankful for.

Or you may prefer a more tangible approach to expressing gratitude. I have an app on my phone called *My Diary*, which I use as a gratitude journal. Whenever I think of something I'm grateful for, I add it. Some days I have several entries, some days I only have one, and some days I skip it altogether. But since I've been keeping my gratitude journal, an amazing thing has happened—I've created a list of reasons to be grateful that I can review any time I feel the dark cloud of negativity looming.

When I'm writing in my gratitude journal, I like to use what I call the "Gratitude Sentence." Here's how it works: Pick a sentence starter like, "I'm grateful for…" or, "I appreciate…" Depending on your faith, you may opt for a more prayerful, "Thank you, God, for…"

Then fill in the blank:

I am grateful for my job.

I appreciate how close I live to work.

I am grateful for the custodian who vacuums my classroom every night so I don't have to.

Thank you, God, for my health so I can teach.

I appreciate the card that Kayla in third period made me.

I appreciate the duplication clerk who always has my work done when I need it.

Thank you, God, for having the Miller boy move to Cleveland.

I'm kidding about the last one (sort of), but you get the picture. We may not always have time to write pages in a journal, but the Gratitude Sentence takes just a moment and allows us to stop, reflect, and express appreciation for our blessings. I encourage you to use a Gratitude Sentence when you feel stressed, anxious, or overwhelmed because it will remind you that not everything is horrible. You can also do it when you are happy, joyous, and bursting with the need to express your appreciation.

Once you get into the habit of identifying and expressing what you're grateful for, you may find that a two-minute gratitude session and maintaining a gratitude journal aren't the best fits for your personality, and that's okay. The method you use to express your gratitude doesn't matter—what *is* important is finding a way that works for you. Here are some more ideas for ways that you can express gratitude:

- Create a gratitude jar. Jot down what you are grateful for and then drop it into the jar.
- Send a thank-you note, letter, or email.
- Make a phone call.

- Pray.
- Commit a random act of kindness. In fact, commit these often and with wild abandon.
- Do something thoughtful, like bringing the secretaries a box of chocolates or some flowers.
- Offer to take a burden off of someone else's shoulders.
- Smile. Ask about someone's life.
- Let your supervisor know he is doing a great job.

Of course, there are always people deserving of praise on your campus. Sometimes a simple "thank you" is enough to let people know that you appreciate their efforts. Other times, you may want to show your gratitude in a more tangible and memorable way. One way I've shown my appreciation to front office staff is by paying for a modest catered lunch. It was nothing fancy—just sandwiches, chips, potato salad, and bottled water—but it showed them that their hard work doesn't go unnoticed. What they do every day makes a difference in my life and makes my job easier; I want them to know I'm grateful for what they do.

One final thought: Don't forget to express gratitude to yourself. You do wonderful things every day as a Zen Teacher, and you should make certain you stop periodically to acknowledge them.

Express self-gratitude by:

- Complimenting yourself.
- Making a list of things you're proud of.
- Giving yourself time to do something for which you have a passion.
- Giving yourself time to do absolutely nothing at all.
- Listing your recent accomplishments.
- Accepting compliments. Take time to really hear them, internalize kind words, and make them a part of who you are. Gracefully accepting compliments is a wildly underappreciated way of showing self-gratitude.

Zen Teachers make it a point every day to reach out to others on campus, to express gratitude, to say thank you, and to count their blessings. Expressing appreciation can only help increase our inner peace and contentment which, in turn, reverberates throughout the class and is inevitably contagious.

ZEN TEACHER ASSIGNMENT

Start and end each day with a Gratitude Sentence.

Detachment

In detachment lies the wisdom of uncertainty
. . . in the wisdom of uncertainty lies the
freedom from our past, from the known,
which is the prison of past conditioning.
—Deepak Chopra

We are taught early on to yearn for the bigger house, to save for (or, worse, charge!) the sixty-inch TV, and make payments on the shiny new car. We have been conditioned to want what we want. But what if we said, "I don't need those things, and that's okay"?

Inconceivable!

What if a teacher said, "Standardized test scores don't matter to me"?

Sacrilege!

Or: "I don't need any new computers or iPads—I'm fine without."

Blasphemy!

Or: "I'm not attached to any particular outcome for this lesson, so let's just see where it goes."

Malpractice!

Or is it?

In the Zen tradition, detachment comes from separating yourself from a desire that if unmet will leave you depressed or disappointed.

By approaching situations with detachment—in other words, with the mindset that things will work out as they are supposed to, no matter what happens—you will walk away feeling more at peace.

But most of us approach life in just the opposite manner.

What if the teacher said, "I have enough right now to teach the students the lessons and skills I need to teach"? What if the teacher focused on teaching his students without obsessing over the "data," which can be spun, tweaked, and twisted until it is nothing but useless fiction, anyway?

This is not to say that excellent teachers will ever eliminate goals and objectives. But by disengaging from an "expected" or "anticipated" outcome, we can create a more authentic learning experience because we haven't invested our mental and emotional energy into an outcome that is "supposed" to happen.

Spiritual guru Dr. Deepak Chopra writes in *The Seven Spiritual Laws of Success*, "You don't give up the intention, and you don't give up the desire. You give up your attachment to the result." Applying this approach in the classroom allows both you and your students to be pleasantly surprised by where lessons take you. In truth, some of the most exciting lessons I've ever taught were the results of telling my classes, "I don't know where this is going, and it might not work. But let's see what happens."

By freeing ourselves from rigid and unyielding expectations, we can engage our students and let our curiosity run wild.

Look at detachment this way: You might say, "If the lesson goes the way I want it to go, excellent! And if it doesn't, that's okay, too." This attitude reduces the weeping and gnashing of teeth the average teacher does in the face of a less-than-stellar lesson and allows him to harness that energy and use it—much more positively—on something even stronger.

You will find that, very often, this kind of lesson creates unforgettable memories for both you and your students and results in what Dave Burgess, author of *Teach Like a Pirate*, calls "life-changing lessons."

By freeing ourselves from rigid and unyielding expectations, we can engage our students and let our curiosity run wild. And when that happens, no matter where we (or our students) end up is part of the plan.

ZEN TEACHER ASSIGNMENT

Think about a situation where you have a clear expectation of what you'd like the outcome to be. And then practice detaching from that outcome by saying, "If that happens, great. But if it doesn't happen, that's okay, too."

And then mean it.

Acceptance

> You can't always get what you want. But if
> you try sometimes, you just might find, you
> get what you need.
> —The Rolling Stones, "You Can't Always Get What You Want"

Show of hands: How many of you struggle with accepting disappointment?

Yeah. Me, too.

Having expectations is unavoidable. We all hope that moments in our lives will turn out a certain way. But even when things go well, they rarely, if ever, go exactly as planned. This truth makes acceptance one of the most helpful skills we can acquire on our journey toward focus, simplicity, and tranquility.

For example, one night, I brought home dinner from the local burger joint for my family. It was early in my role as husband and father, and I was feeling overwhelmed by my new responsibilities and obligations. Having a nice family dinner seemed like a much-needed antidote to a stressful day, and I was looking forward to it. The minute I bit into my burger, however, I knew there was a problem. Maybe it didn't have the extra pickles I requested, or maybe it had mustard when I asked for it without, or maybe they had given me the Cowabunga Burger when I had asked for the Banzai Burger. Without thinking of my behavior (or its consequences), I slammed the burger down on the plate, sighed, and sat back in a huff.

"I don't ask for much," I thought. "Can't they even get one little burger right? After how hard I've been working and all the stress I've been dealing with, don't I at least deserve the burger I want?"

Needless to say, not only did my little tantrum ruin the rest of my night, it also negatively affected everyone else in the house by putting them in a bad mood. In retrospect, not accepting the situation as it was seems positively shameful. Missing pickles? Too much mustard? Who cares? Move on.

Everyone experiences disappointment at some time or another. Maybe the lesson didn't go the way you wanted or your request to attend a conference got denied. Whatever the case, learning to respond to these bumps in life's unpredictable dance with both acceptance and non-judgment, independent of your original expectations, is a skill worth practicing.

I've learned that, as human beings, we have to have emotions, but we don't need to be ruled by them. It's common, though, to try to hang on to good feelings and push away bad ones. But both of those reactions are the very antithesis of acceptance. In contrast, the response of acceptance allows you to stand back, notice your emotions, let them be, and watch them pass serenely through you. Accepting life as it happens does not mean you become a doormat or stop working toward your goals. Instead, it frees you to start where you are, accept what is, and move toward your desired destination with a glad, receptive heart.

In *The Power of Now*, author Eckhart Tolle says, "Surrender is the simple but profound wisdom of yielding to, rather than opposing, the flow of life." And the "surrender" to which he refers sure sounds a lot like acceptance to me.

You will probably never reach a point where you are standing in your doorway, hands on your hips like Superman, with an American flag

> *Accepting life... frees you to start where you are... and move toward your desired destination with a glad, receptive heart.*

waving majestically in the background, and bellowing in your best radio announcer voice, "I have arrived, and I accept what's happening!" It's more likely that you'll stumble along and say, "Wow, I didn't expect that. But I can still make do." Or, "I really want the other thing, but the fact that I got this is pretty good, too."

Acceptance is not so much a destination as an ongoing journey, a method of traveling. And as you travel, you will encounter three primary types of acceptance: acceptance of ourselves, acceptance of others, and acceptance of events.

ACCEPTANCE OF OURSELVES

The media tells us to be something more, better, different. Unhappy with your weight? Try this diet supplement. Unhappy with your appearance? Get liposculpture or a nose job. Very few of us, however, need radical makeovers. We just don't. Learning to accept ourselves for who we are is not a complicated process, but that doesn't make it an easy one, either. We have to overcome years, sometimes decades, of media messages and negative self-talk telling us we need to change.

But what if "I'm too fat" became "I accept my weight and love myself as I am, but I will couple this new acceptance with both moderate and mindful choices about my exercise habits and what I eat"? Over time, you could transform your perceptions—and, ultimately, your self-acceptance.

I've found that one of most difficult parts of teaching is learning to accept one's own limitations. Resisting or fighting against what you perceive as deficits, fuming over the fact that a lesson that didn't rock, lamenting that you don't have the training you need to teach a particular concept with more grace and efficacy, or wishing you had the magic to help you reach that "unreachable" student are all reactions rather than responses of acceptance.

In what ways, if any, do you compare yourself to another teacher who seems to have the perfect classroom or berate yourself for not being "good enough?" How would you feel differently about yourself if you accepted who you are as a teacher and set goals meant to improve your skills, rather than setting goals to be like someone else?

ACCEPTANCE OF OTHERS

Another challenge we face as teachers is struggling with others. Maybe you are irritated by teachers who have a different style than yours, or are disappointed in an administration that doesn't meet your needs, address your concerns, or understand your challenges. Perhaps your students frustrate you when they don't do as you ask or create disturbances in your classes.

Learning to accept others as the complex, contradictory, sometimes infuriating, yet ultimately beautiful creatures they are is a life skill that will benefit us in every area of our lives. If we challenge ourselves to learn this very important skill, even though none of us will learn to like everyone with whom we come in contact, we may end up living a more peaceful life simply because we've learned to accept the nuttiness of humanity in all of its myriad forms.

ACCEPTANCE OF EVENTS

Sometimes, it's not people, but events we have to accept. The unscheduled fire alarm. The spontaneous visit from the principal. The kid who drops to the floor in a dead faint during our lesson (my current count is three in twenty-two years).

When an unexpected event occurs that requires our acceptance, we must step back, separate ourselves from the moment, and view it as a spectator. We have to welcome each event for what it is and open ourselves to what it has to offer.

Here are two activities you can practice to improve your level of acceptance:

THE FIVE-MINUTE ACCEPTANCE TEST

When something unexpected or unwanted happens, try to be present and non-judgmental. Accept the situation and look for the gifts it offers. This process won't take longer than five minutes, so whatever happened will still be there when you're done. But at least you will have attempted to embrace what is, instead of giving in to knee-jerk reactions. Practice with smaller, less important issues (Remember my hamburger story?) and then move up to the issues in your life that might be larger and more difficult to accept.

THE ONE-MINUTE ACCEPTANCE PLAN

Pick one circumstance that is not in sync with your expectations. Find a quiet place and start meditating (or at least breathing). Then say, "This does not meet my expectations. How can I find a way to accept what's happening and see the gifts this situation offers? What can I learn from this circumstance that will take me where I wish to go?" Do this often, and, before long, you will find yourself better able to accept circumstances.

While your journey toward acceptance may not be without missteps, I promise that this practice is worth the effort. In fact, it may well be one of the healthiest habits you can acquire. When you learn to accept failed expectations and common disappointments, you can embrace what life gives you and live a happier life by enjoying what is.

Zen Teacher Assignment

Find an opportunity during your school day when the circumstances are just not turning out the way you hoped. Practice either the Five-Minute Acceptance Test or the One-Step Acceptance Plan (or both). Discover the gifts the situation is offering you (even though it's not what you initially expected or wanted) and then practice embracing what is, instead of what you hoped would be.

Quiet Mind

To a mind that is still,
the whole universe surrenders.
—*Lao Tzu*

Think about those first few moments after you wake up, when you are groggy and feel like you are floating between sleep and awareness. This feeling of relaxed preparedness, this deeply nourishing place between the *doing* of life and the *non-doing* of sleep, is very reminiscent of the Zen state known as Quiet Mind.

When you practice Quiet Mind, you give yourself permission to get in touch with your deeper, truer, purer self. For a moment, time slows as you listen to the rhythm of your soul. Even when thoughts, worries, or concerns arise, in this state of mind, you can accept them with non-judgment and allow them to float through your awareness. Once you acknowledge those thoughts, they dissipate into space, and you return mentally to the peace that comes from focusing on the limitless emptiness and possibility of the calm and quiet present moment.

Through meditation, reflection, silence, stillness, or prayer, we learn to reduce the roar and raucousness until we drop down into a deeper sense of consciousness and have accessed a deeper level of being.

Once you experience Quiet Mind, you will find yourself:

- Listening to your body's rhythms.
- Understanding the vastness of your mind.
- Learning to explore the depths of your heart.
- Discovering the true nature of your soul.

To find your way to Quiet Mind, you must allow yourself time to be still and silent. It could be at the beach, in the mountains, or it could be on the sofa in our living room. Not unlike meditation, which I'll discuss in the next section, Quiet Mind is a state of non-doing. Nothing else should be happening around you, which is why those early morning moments are an ideal time for this Zen Practice.

Pursuing Quiet Mind could even be a daily goal. It takes practice to be comfortable in this place of just noticing and listening, breathing and being, but once you recognize it and know how to get there, the benefits are many. After spending even a few minutes in Quiet Mind, you will be better able to face the chaotic carousel of life renewed, rejuvenated, and refreshed. And once you get the hang of it and find yourself accessing Quiet Mind on a regular basis, it really is a kind of small and beautiful miracle.

ZEN TEACHER ASSIGNMENT

Be still.
Be quiet.
Breathe.
Listen.

MEDITATION
and
MINDFULNESS

Meditation

The purpose of meditation practice is not enlightenment; it is to pay attention even at unextraordinary times,
to be of the present, nothing-but-the-present,
to bear this mindfulness of *now*
into each event of ordinary life.
—*Peter Matthiessen, The Snow Leopard*

Once, while at the dentist's office having a cavity filled, the sound emanating from the drill became especially high-pitched and the pressure on my tooth particularly uncomfortable. I knew that focusing on my discomfort would only increase it, so I decided to notice my environment and take stock of the rest of my body's physical condition. I saw the fluorescent lights over me burning, I felt myself leaning back in the chair, and I heard the evening news blasting from the nearby TV. My arms and legs were tight, my hands gripping the chair's armrests.

While the doctor seemed to be up to his elbows in my mouth, I got in touch with my breathing, and I took several deep, cleansing breaths through my nose. Then I found a stain on the ceiling, made it my focal point, emptied my mind, focused on my breathing, stayed present in the moment, and began meditating.

Getting the filling was still no picnic, but I was immediately able to relax and better handle the pressure and the drilling. The entire process

Meditation gives us the luxury of focusing on one thing at a time so that we can see it both accurately and with intention.

took less than five minutes, but the discovery that I could clear my mind and relax my body even in uncomfortable circumstances felt liberating.

And that is meditation in its simplest form.

In *The Relaxation & Stress Reduction Workbook*, the authors describe meditation as "the practice of attempting to focus your attention on one thing at a time." That is not exactly a popular concept in our must-be-productive culture, but meditating can be an excellent way for us to relax and dissipate the stress that inevitably builds up at home and in the classroom.

Too many of us feel as if we are not effective unless we are simultaneously answering questions, hole-punching papers, correcting quizzes, ordering supplies, or handing out bathroom passes. But meditation gives us the luxury of focusing on one thing at a time so that we can see it both accurately and with intention.

Some of the most fundamental approaches to meditation are also some of its greatest advantages: clearing our mind of distractions, focusing on our breathing so we can appreciate what it means to live, and staying present in the moment to remind us that this is the only moment that matters. Meditation also has clear and scientifically proven health benefits. According to WebMD, for example, Dr. Charles L. Raison, clinical director of the Mind-Body Program at Emory University School of Medicine, participated in a study that indicated that both physical and emotional stress could be reduced through the regular practice of meditation. In the study, he found that "people who meditated regularly for six weeks showed less activation of their immune systems and less emotional distress when they were put in a stressful situation."

As you read through some of the chapters in this section with titles such as "Meditation," " Mindfulness," "Present Moment Awareness," and "Paying Attention," you will notice that although they are distinct concepts with their own focuses and approaches, they also share certain similarities that make them an integrated part of a meditation/mindfulness experience when it comes to teaching you how to be present in your life.

Gazing Meditation

If you've ever taken a birthing class, you understand the nature (and benefits) of finding a focal point and then using it to focus your breathing, your attention, and your thoughts. This is a gazing meditation, and it's worth noting that performing it need not result in the birth of a baby.

The first step is choosing a focal point. I've known people to use everything from a stuffed animal to a candle to a crumpled bakery bag of leftover donuts—anything will work. Next, draw your attention to your breathing and get in touch with your breath impulse. While gazing at your focal point, concentrate on the rhythm of your breathing and make attempts to clear your mind. Tune out distractions, ignore noises, and keep your attention on your focal point. Soon, you will notice that random thoughts will start to show up—"My nose itches," "I need to get milk at the grocery store," "The dog needs flea medicine," "What was really going on between Mr. Kincaid and Shirley Partridge?" When those thoughts seep into your consciousness, acknowledge that they are there and let them slip out of the other side of your mind. More will come, so let them come and go as well. Then allow your gaze to stay on your focal point and reconnect with your breath impulse.

That's all there is to it. This process can be as long or as short as the time you've set aside for it, whether that is five minutes or two hours.

Mantra Meditation

You have probably seen movies and television shows with people chanting or humming *om* while they meditate. *Om* is just one example of a mantra, albeit an ancient one, but any word or phrase that you say aloud or in your head while you're meditating can be a mantra, as long as that word or phrase keeps you focused on your breathing and the present moment.

Meditation for Wimps author Miriam Austin gives us several options for mantra-style meditation. One method for employing the mantra is to focus on your breath, inhale, and then exhale on a mantra. Austin suggests the following statements:

- "May I be free from suffering."
- "May I be at peace."
- "May I be full of confidence."

Or even repeating a phrase such as:

- "I am patience. I am patience. I am patience."
- "I calm my anger." (Said once while inhaling and once while exhaling.)

I think the last two can be particularly handy for both teachers and parents.

Austin also says you can employ lovingkindness and meditate with your focus on others. She suggests focusing on a specific person and inhaling and exhaling on the following concepts:

- "May you be free from suffering."
- "May you be full of joy."

From a spiritual standpoint, it's easy to see how meditation is similar to prayer, but what sets meditation apart is the fact that it focuses your thoughts and intentions on a single idea, desired outcome, or state of being. For example, I have personally benefited from simply inhaling on the word "peace" and exhaling on the word "tranquility." While it isn't necessarily a request made to God, it can be a practice for clearing the mind enough so it can focus on more spiritual concepts.

Stray thoughts will make every attempt to interfere with your concentration and distract you while you meditate. Don't let them. Each time you realize your mind is wandering, acknowledge the stray thoughts, allow them to pass through your mind, and then return to your meditation. At first, it will be difficult not to dwell on them or chastise yourself for having them, but one of meditation's best qualities is that it is non-judgmental. Whatever is happening is exactly what is happening; it is neither good nor bad but should be accepted because it simply is.

No matter how much or how little time you have, you can find peace and relaxation in your classroom, at home, in your car, or wherever you are.

Meditation is simply sitting and breathing. That's it.

I can hear some of you saying, "There must be more to it than that."

Nope. Just sit and breathe.

And then you say, "But surely, that can't be all. Don't I have to press a button, sign a paper, click a link, or look at a screen?"

To which I reply, "Nope. Just sit and breathe."

And you say, "But. . ."

And I say, "*Shhhh—.*"

Sit.

Breathe.

That's it.

Now you try it.

See? Wasn't that nice?

Zen Teacher Assignment

Practice a simple meditation. Sit comfortably, and then, breathing naturally, begin to focus on the nature of your breath. Notice the rhythm and impulse of your breathing. Only breathe when you feel the impulse. You may have your eyes opened or closed, whatever best allows you to focus on your breathing.

As thoughts come, acknowledge them and then let them flow right out of the other side of your mind. Return your focus to your breath impulse. Thoughts are not the enemy but more like shooting stars. They will come and go, arcing their way across the universe of your mind, and that's fine—just notice them without judgment or attachment. Just because thoughts run through the river of our minds doesn't mean we have to jump in the current for a swim.

Walking Meditation

When I began taking early morning walks more than a year ago, I desperately needed to get in shape (and I was kind of hoping I would lose some weight along the way). I would wake up at 5 a.m. every day, and, after cursing the gods and the darkness, I would put on my sweatpants, sweatshirt, sneakers, and red, knit watch cap.

Before long, I began to notice that not only was I really enjoying my morning walk, but I was actually looking forward to it—I mean, *really* looking forward to it. It became my time to enjoy nature, go slowly, find stillness, reflect on life, and create a sense of peace in my spirit. Once I entered the "maintenance" phase of my fitness and weight loss, I decided that I would continue walking the same route: slowly, mindfully, and with a great sense of being present.

I hadn't felt that peaceful and relaxed in years.

THE HOW-TOS OF WALKING MEDITATION

Walking can be a form of meditation and offers the added benefit of physical activity. It's best to do your walking meditation outdoors to give yourself space to roam and your mind a break from noise and clutter. Whether it's around the block, in a nearby park, or on a local trail, research shows that nature breaks can improve performance, particularly when you're under stress. But if the weather outside isn't suitable for a stroll, you may also try walking around your living room, bedroom, family room, garage, basement, or even on a treadmill.

Start by noticing your body and how it feels. Stand there. Which areas feel most comfortable? Do you notice tension? If so, where? Do you need to stretch or massage anything before beginning?

After a quick assessment of your body, you're ready to begin. I have outlined some steps to follow for a basic walking meditation, but feel free to modify them depending on what works for you:

1. *Focus on your breathing.* Breathe normally and become aware of the organic rhythm of your breaths.

2. *Begin walking as you normally would.* Notice your footfalls. Become aware of how your heel touches the ground followed by the rest of your foot. Walk as slowly or as quickly as comes natural to you.

3. *As you walk, begin to sense each part of your body*—your feet, ankles, knees, hips, pelvis, belly, chest, back, neck, and head. What feels good? Are you experiencing discomfort? Become aware of your body's natural state and its inherent rhythms. Feel any aches and pains. Feel your heart pumping.

4. *Let thoughts come and go.* If you find yourself thinking, acknowledge the thought and let it flow out of your mind. Then refocus on your body, the walking, and the present moment.

5. *Notice your feelings.* Are you tired? Happy? Irritated? Relaxed?

6. *Pay attention to your surroundings.* If you are outside, do you hear birds, voices, or traffic? If you are inside, do you hear your feet hit the carpet? Is the TV on? Do you hear a pet or family member in the next room? Use your senses. What do you see? Hear? Smell?

7. *There is no judgment in a walking meditation.* Nothing is good or bad—it just is. Enjoy the chance to just be.

8. *Continue to walk naturally* with a relaxed, open, and aware state of mind.

9. *When you feel you're done, come to a natural standing position.* Take a final assessment of your surroundings and your body.

A walking meditation can certainly be a formal event, but it can also be a more spontaneous experience as well. Even short walks from the school building to your car in the parking lot can create a moment of meditation and mindfulness.

When I arrive at school in the morning, for example, I like to get out of my car, stand next to it for a second, and just look at the school, the walkway, the sky, and the mountains. Just for a moment, I focus on my breathing and embrace the turning world before I start my workday. Then I try to make my walk from the car to the office a deeply meditative experience. It's a very beautiful, rewarding, and ultimately relaxing start to my teaching day.

When could you fit a walking meditation into your day? Could you walk down the hallway focused on your breathing during the six- or seven-minute passing period? Could you take a five- or ten-minute walk during recess or break? Could you devote fifteen minutes twice a week—say, Tuesdays and Thursdays during lunch or a free period—to a walking meditation?

The amazing thing is that you can do a walking meditation any time you walk. Stillness is great, powerful, and even essential, but it was revelatory for me to hear that I could still find that sense of peace and tranquility through movement, through doing.

ZEN TEACHER ASSIGNMENT

Take a walk. As you walk, use your senses to experience what is happening around you. Notice thoughts you may have and allow them to float right on by so that they don't interrupt your presence in the moment.

When you're done, do a quick physical and emotional assessment.

How does your body feel?

What are you thinking or feeling?

Are you calmer?

Do you feel more peaceful?

Try this at home when you want to get away, even for a few minutes. Try it at school, even if it's just a quick walk from the classroom to the office.

Mindfulness

When we commit ourselves to paying attention in an open way . . . we have a chance to free ourselves from the straightjacket of unconsciousness.
—Jon Kabat-Zinn, *Wherever You Go, There You Are*

You're finally home from work and ready to kick back and relax in your house—your sanctuary from the world. But when you open the door, you are greeted by the baby crying, the phone ringing, the dog hurling on the carpet, and the pots on the stove bubbling over to create a gelatinous mess on the counter.

Before you do something that will make you the top story on the eleven o'clock news, stop where you are and breathe. Recognize that this moment is beautiful and complete. Realize that you will enjoy it much more if you accept it as it is and detach from any further expectation as to how it should be.

Of course, you're thinking, "Listen, Einstein, if I could stop and breathe during these moments, I wouldn't be as stressed as I am." And you're right. You can't stop moments like these from happening, but you can learn how to handle them so they will be easier to endure. That's where mindfulness can help.

Mindfulness, which can actually be used as a form of meditation all by itself, is the conscious knowledge that this moment is all you have, and it is neither good nor bad. However, being present for it requires using all of your senses, intention, and awareness. When you approach life from a place of mindfulness, everything is happening exactly as it should and should be accepted as it is. Take a moment and think about how liberating it would be to just live inside a moment free of expectations, judgment, and failure.

The moment just is. That's the magic of mindfulness.

That's not to say every single moment of your life will be rainbows, unicorns, and text messages from Sandra Bullock (clearly, that last one was just for me, but you see my point) because it won't. Rather, your sense of the present—and its perfection as the universe meant it to be—can help experience the now. "Step into the unknown," Deepak Chopra says, "and you become open to all possibilities."

It's ridiculously easy to get caught up in what has happened and what could happen. Focused on the future or the past, we lose the magic of the moment that is right in front of us. For example, have you ever driven to school and, once you got there, thought about the drive and could not recall a single moment? Part of the grace and purity of mindfulness is that it reduces our life from a ginormous, amorphous blob into small, manageable pieces—this moment and then this one—and forces us to fully engage in and focus on the present.

Unfortunately, we hardly ever structure our lives to focus on a single moment. We are distracted, fragmented, and unfocused. We multi-task. We lament the past and worry about the future. We fret about the doctor's appointment, the children's grades, the bills we have to pay, all the while missing the moment, and really, our lives.

*The moment just is.
That's the magic of mindfulness.*

We miss so many gifts each day when we power through without stopping to notice the world's beauty and grandeur. But what would it look like if we were to stop? To disconnect from the rat race and give ourselves enough quiet time to focus on this very moment?

It might look something like this:

1. Stop.
2. Get in touch with the rhythm of your breathing.
3. Look around.
4. What do you see?
5. What do you smell?
6. What do you hear?
7. Do not judge.
8. Expect nothing.
9. Merely notice what you notice.
10. Catalog the physical sensations of your body. Are you hot? Cold? Do you itch somewhere? Do you feel any pain or discomfort?
11. Just sit in acceptance and experience.
12. Return to your life with a renewed sense of energy and rejuvenation.

A mindful experience can ground you in your own reality when the rest of the world has gone crazy. If you listen carefully, it can also offer alternatives to the lunacy. As mindfulness expert and author of *Wherever You Go, There You Are: Mindfulness Meditation in Everyday Life,* Jon Kabat-Zinn, PhD, says, "When we commit ourselves to paying attention in an open way, without falling prey to our own likes and dislikes, opinions and prejudices, projections and expectations, new possibilities open up and we have a chance to free ourselves from the straightjacket of unconsciousness."

Mindfulness can be applied to every area of your life, from washing your hands to doing the dishes to teaching. The benefits of mindfulness in the classroom are without end. Learning to focus on what is immediately happening is something excellent teachers have always done.

Imagine being mindful—in other words, totally present—in the lesson you teach today. What would that look like? Would you approach the material differently? The students? Yourself? How would a mindful approach affect the overall vibe in your classroom?

Imagine the power, the focus.

Imagine how it would increase the peace and energy of the experience.

Once you have a little practice just living in the moment, things get easier, they become simpler—and even more enjoyable. The newfound inner quiet allows you to appreciate, recognize, and embrace the special moments life offers. In the end, a mindful mindset will pay great dividends; all those gifts you previously rushed past will become a cherished part of your daily life.

Zen Teacher Assignment

Take a walk in your neighborhood and pay attention to your surroundings. Use your senses. Listen to the dogs barking, the children laughing, and the smoky smell of a neighbor grilling. See the leaves on the trees, the sun, the sky, and the moon. It's all there, just waiting for you.

Present Moment Awareness

As I approached a hill I climb every morning on my daily walk around my San Diego neighborhood, something made me look up.

The sky was still dark, but it was completely clear. A multitude of stars, like silver pinpricks in a giant sheet of black velvet, shimmered near a small fist of bone-white moon. On the left, I saw a constellation I could not name, and, to my right, shone the gorgeous, and more easily recognizable, Big Dipper. The birds around me called to each other as they woke. A slight breeze ruffled the hair on my arm. To an onlooker, I might have looked as if I were having a petit mal seizure. Nevertheless, I stood there, looking up, breathing, and experiencing.

Present Moment Awareness, which is a form of mindfulness, invites us to use our senses to experience each moment of our lives with a fresh and involved perspective, where we learn to step into and really live in the moment. At any time, day or night. It asks us to stop and really see, hear, taste, touch, and smell what is around us and reflect on what is actually happening, instead ignoring and dismissing the million activities that we scuttle through, zombie-like, every day. Think of it this way: if mindfulness is the car you're driving in, Present Moment Awareness is the engine that makes it run.

With every new gadget created to make our lives easier, we are pulled further into a faster-paced world with more needless activity—whether it's updating our Facebook status or posting a picture of our Starbucks' Venti mocha on Instagram. In our haste, we rarely ask ourselves what is happening around us, and even more frightening, never stop to ask if this is how we want to spend our finite time on this big blue marble.

Present Moment Awareness, however, offers us the chance to step off the carousel of life—if only for a moment—to experience and appreciate the sensory stimuli whizzing by us, while our eyes are glued to our phones, our ears plugged with earbuds. As a more focused state of mind,

Present Moment Awareness asks us to be conscious of our world, our lifestyle, and our choices.

In the old days, for example, I would eat whatever I could get my hands on. In addition to the standard three meals a day, I snacked constantly on potato chips, trail mix, M&M's, ice cream with caramel sauce and whipped cream—whatever was on the counter, in the cupboard, or in the fridge. Most nights I would end with my all-time favorite snack: a giant bowl of hot, buttered popcorn. Truth be told, I am an emotional eater. I would eat when I celebrated, when I was depressed, and when I was bored, never thinking about what I was doing.

When I decided to lose weight, I knew diets wouldn't work because, for me, the only thing worse than feeling overweight was feeling deprived. So I came up with a new solution: mindfulness in the present moment.

One day I simply started paying attention and being present during my eating binges. It was never about eating fewer calories but about noticing the calories. I asked myself, "Is this where I want this day's calories to come from? Should I wait until later? Eat something else altogether? Should I trade the donut for an apple? Just say no completely and walk away? Do I want this snack and popcorn later?"

Suddenly, that extra handful of M&M's didn't seem so important.

Present Moment Awareness asks us to be conscious of our world, our lifestyle, and our choices.

This mindfulness approach is not just about food or drink but the fact that you can be present in your own life during any moment, any activity, any discipline. Though it stems from a Zen Practice that is centuries old, Present Moment Awareness is now used to create peace and tranquility in troubled students, reduce discomfort, stress, and tension, and even to teach patients how to deal with chronic pain.

As teachers, Present Moment Awareness helps us step outside the chaos created by mindless meetings, new curricula, and everyday noise. It allows us, as the lead learners in our own classrooms, to consciously navigate where our ships are headed and decide on the nature and purpose of our missions.

Think for a moment about your current lesson plan. Are you doing it without conscious thought because you've done it a million times? Or is it time to stop and ask yourself, "Is this the best way to present *Romeo and Juliet*?" The Pythagorean theorem? The Magna Carta?

That kind of presence is truly empowering.

The Zen Teacher doesn't just ask, "Why am I eating this hot fudge sundae?" He asks, "Why am I doing this worksheet, this lesson, this book?"

And as a bonus, it doesn't hurt to stop and look at the stars once in a while, either.

ZEN TEACHER ASSIGNMENT

At least once today, remind yourself to stop, use your senses, and be present in the moment staring you in face. What do you see, hear, and smell? How can you focus on the present to intensify the joy in your life and experience the gift of your existence? It only takes a moment to be present. Practice being mindful and use Present Moment Awareness during the most mundane activities in life, as well as the most exciting. No moment in life is worth not being there for. Trust me, the practice is worth it.

Watching The River Flow

In her book *The Long, Steep Path*, Catherine Ryan Hyde paraphrases Heraclitus when she writes, "You can never step twice into the same stream." Even when I read this quote for the first time, the meaning behind it took my breath away. Instantly, I understood how much I had been taking for granted, how much I had failed to see, to realize, to know. As if a light switch flipped, I suddenly saw how routine and mundane my days had become by assuming that, merely because I've been somewhere before, there couldn't possibly be anything new to experience.

I was wrong.

Totally and completely wrong.

It was liberating to realize that, no matter how many times I go somewhere, even if it is every day, there are new things to see, to experience, and to learn. When I realized I could see a familiar place anew, the world widened for me about a million percent.

After reading Hyde's essay, I remember being in my classroom—a place I'd lived Monday through Friday for the past two decades—and I put down her book and walked outside the classroom door, just to see what was there. In some ways, it was the same old sidewalk, the same old greenbelt, and the same old tree. But armed with my new understanding of this being a "stream" in my life that I can never step in twice, I also saw new things. I heard bees buzzing around the low-hanging branches, I saw the brown spots where the grass had been eaten away by both time and the footfalls of teenagers, I was horrified by the ancient knots of old gum on the sidewalk that had fossilized into an ugly black mosaic.

Each time I step outside my classroom now, I try to see the "stream" as fresh and new—because it is. Even as I write this at my desk and take a break to go outside, I see the way the afternoon sunlight falls at a slant on the building across the grass, I watch the leaves' shadows dance on the sidewalk, and I hear students' laughter echoing in the hallways.

Every time I step out, I see something new.

Same stream. New experience.

Interestingly, the same truth can be applied to your students as well. Each day that they arrive in your classroom, they are different. The time that has passed since you last encountered them has changed not only you but also them. And these changes can be intriguing, exciting, profound, and, frankly, these daily differences make it ridiculous for you to hold yesterday against them. In essence, you're all in a new stream together.

But the classroom is not your only stream. After work tonight, look around as you prepare dinner or go through the evening ritual of putting the children to bed. You've been in your house a million times, and you tell yourself you know every nook and cranny. But do you really?

> "You can never step twice into the same stream."

I guarantee that, if you were to look closely, you would see new details of your old, "boring" life; you would discover new truths and new wonders, all because you can't step into the same stream twice.

Learning to view the places where you spend your life as places of awe, wonder, and infinite possibility will help you experience that contentment, as you come to realize there is something new in every moment of our life. Even Bob Dylan, who sang, "I just sit here so contentedly and watch the river flow," apparently understood this feeling. Whether you see it as a river or a stream hardly matters; it's seeing the new and unique things in the familiar and comfortable current that will keep you present and make you appreciate how unique each moment of life can be."

Zen Teacher Assignment

When you walk into your classroom in the morning, take a moment and write down ten things that you see that are new to you—things that you just haven't noticed recently because you've been taking that space for granted. Then do the same thing the next day, but remember that the ten things have to be different from the ones you wrote down first. Then do it that night in your home. Marvel at the newness of the various streams of your life.

Paying Attention

Have you ever taken a walk on a street you've traveled a million times before, only to say, "I didn't know that was there"? But what if you stopped for a moment and noticed—really noticed—what is around you? If you were to do that, you might find yourself experiencing a sense of joy and sensory overload that rivals a day at Disneyland. The truth is that, every day, we are bombarded with stimuli, and, rather than trying to pay attention to it all, we tune out, when we should be doing the exact opposite.

I majored in drama in college and spent more than two years pursuing acting in Los Angeles. One of the unexpected benefits of training to be an actor and a writer is that I learned to pay attention to details and to observe life as it takes place. Think of the great actors and actresses, the De Niros and Streeps of the silver screen. Almost without exception, the more they pay attention to the moment, the better their performance. Actors are conditioned to pay attention to their scene partner, focus on the moment, and be present, undistracted by memories, worries, or fears.

When we pay attention to something, we use our senses intensely and with intention. However, our society's twenty-first-century quirks have stifled our ability to do this. Most of us walk through the world preoccupied with worry and regret, neither of which we can actively affect. Or we are glued to our devices, as if they are talismans holding answers. Our best shot at finding the answers we're seeking, though, is by raising our heads and just looking at what's right in front of us.

Paying deep, genuine attention is not something our culture rewards. While making dinner, we are writing lesson plans. While walking the dog, we are rehearsing an upcoming phone call to our colleague about how he missed a deadline. While taking a shower to let the water soothe our sore muscles, we are fretting about how we are going to pay for the water. But it does not have to be that way.

Once again, one of the first steps we can take in focusing our attention is reinvigorating our five senses. Ask yourself these questions:

- What do I see?
- What do I hear?
- What do I smell?
- What do I feel?
- What do I taste?
- What specific things do I notice?
- Who else is around?
- How does my body feel right now?

Our answers to these questions bring us into the beauty of our own reality and allow us to experience what is actually happening. And the best part is, you can ask yourself those questions anytime, anywhere.

Even right now. Try it.

I'll wait.

Okay. Though paying close attention to something can take energy, some moments of our lives may seem boring, average, or bland and unworthy of recognition. But that's probably because we just are not looking hard enough at the beauty, possibility, and potential before us. We must learn to be attentive, even to the mundane, uninteresting moments in our lives.

Paying attention is about noticing the details in life. In fiction, the truthful detail can sell the story. In poetry, the exacting detail can move a person to feel. In comedy, the telling detail can cause a joke to absolutely kill. As Zen Teachers, our goal is to find the right details and to nurture, celebrate, and, most importantly, recognize and acknowledge them. We need to discover what makes this moment . . . *this* moment.

Not too long ago, for example, I had occasion to walk from my classroom to the office. Instead of worrying about my afternoon classes, next semester's core literature choices, or how the right front headlight of my car had recently died, I tried my best to simply notice my surroundings, be in the moment, and pay attention to the details of my walk. Unencumbered by other thoughts, I noticed: a gaggle of students crossing the quad, chatting and texting, laughing and squealing, pushing and shoving; the buzz of table saws and boisterous conversation (as well as a few expletives) coming from the woodshop class; a puddle on the concrete by the cafeteria, reflecting the lunch tables; and the humming of the air conditioner as I re-entered my class, cooling the room.

It was these specific and particular details, the kind of details that we often ignore or take for granted, that made the moment come alive for me and allowed me to be a present participant in my own life.

Opportunities like this exist every day, especially in our classrooms. As teachers, the rhythm and chemistry of the day change often, even within the course of a few moments, and we are provided with countless reasons to pay attention to people, objects, events, and patterns. Pay attention to the details and you'll find the moment.

> *Why is Veronica sleeping?*
> *What is Louie going to do with that wad of paper in his hand?*
> *When did I run out of glue sticks?*
> *Why does Marco look so sad?*
> *Should I say something to Kylie and Emily, lifelong best friends, as they do not seem to be speaking to each other?*

And so on…

And believe me, I recognize the irony. With lesson plans to write, papers to grade, and a truckload of students who all have different needs, teachers struggle to "pay attention" with no rush, no burden, and no criticism. But even there, we should have no judgment. It's a process and we need to be kind to ourselves.

By focusing on the immediate moment (instead of allowing ourselves to be preoccupied by random, irrelevant thoughts) and using our senses (instead of ignoring our environments), we can meaningfully increase our sense of joy for a world that exists around us all day, every day—if we only care enough to look.

ZEN TEACHER ASSIGNMENT

Pick a single situation—whether it's balancing your checkbook, writing a blog post, explaining a concept to your students, vacuuming your family room, or listening to your child's stories from his day—and pay close attention. Notice what's really happening. See what's really there. And do it without the idea that it needs to be anything other than what it is.

Everyday Mindfulness

Each moment is a gift, and we owe it to ourselves to be conscious of that gift as it happens. No activity or experience should be exempt from our taking notice or being present with it. Even the most repetitive, mundane acts, such as paying the bills, shaving, or taking a breath can be made more "real" by being present as they take place. In these instances, we must resist the temptation to let these singular moments merely pass by unnoticed and, instead, embrace them and luxuriate in the beauty they have to offer.

If you think about it, opportunities to practice mindfulness and be appreciative present themselves to us during each and every activity, each and every day, even before we step foot out of our house. And yet we often ignore the chances we have to tune in to the gift of each occurrence, even when these occurrences have to happen anyway.

Let's look at three activities that happen before we go to work in the morning: showering, eating breakfast, and driving to work. Each gives us the chance to be more aware of life's moments.

SHOWERING

Many people find a sense of peace and tranquility taking a long, hot bath after a trying day. But even those who take a more workman-like, functional shower every morning before heading off to the classroom are missing out on an opportunity to open their senses to a great opportunity to truly feel alive. A shower is a necessary and ordinary part of our lives that always (or almost always) happens when we're alone. As such, it is an opportunity to be present—without distraction.

Imagine what would happen if you were to step into the shower and feel your hand on the faucet, breathe as the warm water cascades down your neck and shoulders, and feel the soft terry cloth of the towel as it slips through your fingers and you dry your body?

How much more relaxed would you be?

How much better would you feel?

Would you begin your day in a better place?

Bathing is an incredibly sensual experience, and if we could tap into at least some of that sensuality, imagine how much more alive we would feel as we readied for our day. Just think how much richer, deeper, and more profound our life experience would be simply by choosing to be mindful as we bathed.

Eating Breakfast

Even though I rarely eat more than a simple bowl of cereal for breakfast, I'm trying to break myself of the habit of using my time while eating to scroll through yet another useless social media feed or sneak in another unnecessary email check. I'm reminding myself that I should not only be tasting, but actually enjoying, the cereal on my taste buds, whether it's Lucky Charms, Raisin Bran, or just a humble bowl of Cheerios.

And whether you choose to have a yogurt, a bagel, a smoothie, or even if you just down a few grapes as you grab your purse or briefcase and head for the door, you can break your morning fast in a thoughtful way that takes advantage of your five senses. With practice, you will learn to be present and make your morning meal a more meditative and centering experience that prepares you for the day ahead.

Driving To Work

Since I've been taking the same route to work for over two decades, it shouldn't be too surprising that I often arrive at work with virtually no recollection of the drive I made to get there. Typically, I shrug it off by reassuring myself that this time lapse happens to everyone and that it's completely normal. But if I'm being honest, my lack of memory of these drives can be quite unsettling. Our morning commute is one of those times when it's exceptionally easy to become dangerously disconnected and miss what life has to offer.

On the other hand, if I'm alive and mindful and present, there is a moment in my drive every morning that can be truly glorious. At one point, the freeway rises up over a summit, and, once the summit is cleared, the view can be breathtaking. On clear days, I can see an expansive blue sky, white puffy clouds inching across the horizon and, on the far side of this glorious vista, an overlay of several small mountain ranges that vary in color, from brown to blue to purple. And as if that weren't magical enough, there, spread across the valley, are the tiny houses, streets, and stores of the town I grew up in.

This view frequently is all it takes to wake me up, and I often find myself in awe of its beauty.

Ask yourself: "Where is the beauty in my commute? What do I pass by every day that, if I stopped to notice it, would add a sense of magic and wonder to my life?" I challenge you to look for it; I guarantee you that moment of beauty and awe is there.

What do you do every day that could add a sense of magic and wonder to your life?

So in the end, could there be three more mundane, routine activities to start your day off than showering, eating, and driving to work? Could there be three more common responsibilities in which we must partake? Could there be three more simple and easy opportunities for us to add a little beauty, peace, and serenity to our lives? I doubt it.

Of course, you could find three more activities at work where everyday mindfulness would come in handy, three more activities after work where a little extra presence will help relax you, and three more activities before going to bed where peace is just waiting for you.

It isn't difficult to find them.

What takes practice is recognizing and acting on them.

And at this point, you may be asking if there is a single moment where being mindful and more present wouldn't help. But by now, I suspect you already know the answer, don't you?

ZEN TEACHER ASSIGNMENT

Choose one of the three areas mentioned above—showering, eating breakfast, or driving to work—and create a mindful experience around it. Be present. Use your senses. Take stock of what's happening. Pay attention to the details and fully experience it. Consciously decide that you will make it a great and powerful start to your day.

Be Here Now

In 1971, counterculture leader and former Harvard psychologist Ram Dass wrote a book called *Be Here Now*, a manifesto celebrating the benefits of living in the present moment. Since then, the expression, "be here now," has become a catchphrase for the Zen-inspired path and a lifestyle for those seeking fulfillment and peace.

Let's take a look at what "be here now" really means.

BE

Hamlet's immortal line, "To be or not to be," makes me wonder if he was part Zen Master. To be is to exist, and many of us are not as present as we should be in our own existence. Instead, we spend our time regretting the past or worrying about the future, rather than focusing on the beauty sitting right before us. Though English teachers often ask us to avoid it, we should embrace *to be*; we should invite it into our being, accept it, and even revel in it. When you're in your home, be in your home. When you're in your classroom, be in your classroom. Being is the universe's greatest gift, and it deserves to celebrated, experienced, and most of all, treated with respect.

HERE

Learning from the past and planning for the future are important, but trying to live in the past or future isn't possible, and our attempts to do so waste our precious lives. Yet many of us spend our days re-living events that we'll never be able to change. We also fret over a future that hasn't happened yet, nor will it ever, because the moment that future arrives, it's no longer the future, but the present.

So often we try to be somewhere else, re-living the awkward parent-teacher conference from last Tuesday or rehearsing our upcoming meeting with the principal, and yet you can only be where you are, and where you are is here. But if you go over there, then there will suddenly and magically be here. In other words, there is only ever *here* because we can only be one place at a time.

"Zen does not confuse spirituality with thinking about God while one is peeling potatoes," says Alan Watts, a writer and Zen philosopher. "Zen spirituality is just to peel the potatoes."

Now

Yesterday and tomorrow only exist in our minds. Each moment of our life is stitched together with the last and is a link in the eternal chain we call "now." So the question (and the quest) becomes: How can you more deeply appreciate, accept, and participate in each now, without getting caught up in what happened in a previous now or what might happen in a future now?

One of the ironies for us as teachers is that we must both reflect on and prepare for the next unit while teaching the current one. But that dynamic makes it even more imperative for us to cultivate the practice of being present in the now of our current students, current lesson, and current moment.

Whenever you feel stressed or paralyzed by the unrelenting, unending dysfunction of the education machine, give yourself permission to stop, breathe, detach from unnecessary expectations and judgments, and remind yourself to just

be

here

now.

Intention

Whether it is eating a tuna sandwich for lunch, putting away the spades and gloves after working in the garden, washing the dishes, or doing a load of laundry, when we act with intention—making ourselves aware of what we are doing and choosing to behave in harmony with our personal values and beliefs—we experience each task, no matter how mundane it is. As a result, every activity in which we partake offers us the opportunity to truly live.

You may know people who sleepwalk through life and perform the dysfunctional judo of simply reacting to circumstances. You may know them, but you probably don't want to be one of them. We can avoid that fate when we live intentionally, when we live with a purpose. Think of each intention as a star in your own personal sky that makes up the universe of your life.

In the classroom, the key to acting with intention is deciding what you want to have happen. We should not resort to reactive lurches at the mercy of administrative, district, or even state mandates. Instead, we can initiate a carefully considered and intentional choice about what our values are, about what our priorities are, about what our goals might be. And then do whatever it takes to get there.

Don't get me wrong; you may very well have to operate under certain guidelines, even requirements, but the fact of the matter is that you are the boss. I always find it exhilarating (and as scary as hell) to remember that what happens in my classroom is, by and large, up to me. The buck stops at my desk. I can't help but teach through the prism of my personal point of view and my idiosyncratic choices. So really, I have a professional obligation to ensure that I act with intention and choose with mindful awareness what my students encounter during their adventure within the four walls of my classroom.

When we're talking about goals, professional or personal, there are three basic steps to acting with intention:

1.   Ask yourself, "What do I want?"
2.   Then ask, "What are the steps to getting there?"
3.   Then take the first step. And then the second. Then the third. And so on . . .

And just as we must be intentional about our goals, we must also be intentional about achieving peace and equanimity. We must learn to choose to pursue our sense of Zen, otherwise the world will fill the space of our indecision with disruption and distraction.

In my house, for example, the family calendar runs everything. If something is on the calendar, it happens. I choose my times of rest and relaxation intentionally and put them in ink right in the middle of the appropriate white square.

> In the classroom, the key to acting with intention is deciding what you want to have happen.

At first glance, it may seem impossible to act with both intention and detachment, but it's not. You can always set goals with intention, make a choice about what you would like to have happen in your life, but then act with a peaceful detachment from pre-determined outcomes, ready to go wherever the road takes you and accept whatever life throws at you. The two do not have to be contradictory. You'll be much happier if you think of it less as a discrepancy and more of a dance. Creating a plan, scheduling your time appropriately, and then being open to life's twists and turns, instead of being discouraged by them, will allow you to make the most of each moment.

ZEN TEACHER ASSIGNMENT

Start small. Choose one decision you have to make today and DO NOT leave it up to chance, randomness, or serendipity. It can be: "What will I wear to school today?" "Which math problems will I assign?" "What restaurant will we have dinner at tonight?" "What is my most important academic goal this semester?" Send out your intention into the universe and make it a point to make a conscious decision to ask, "What do I want?" and "How can I get there?" And then let it go and leave the rest up to the universe.

Rituals

For a long time, I fought the idea of rituals. I let my days unfold any old way they wanted, certain I was living a serendipitous, Bohemian existence. My nose was raised high, proud that my life was spontaneous. I refused to be a slave, a time-clock-punching, working-class drone whose every second was scheduled to the *nth* degree and who had no time to welcome an unplanned, unpredictable future.

What a drama queen.

Rituals—the right rituals, anyway—create balance and help us focus our attention on the moment in a way that an unplanned, unstructured life cannot. Let's be clear, though: I'm not talking about bizarre religious rituals that involve small dolls, long needles, and that guy or girl you dated in eleventh grade. Although they may have religious origins or overtones, rituals have given meaning to people's lives for centuries, regardless of their belief systems.

For our purposes, a ritual refers to creating some small and periodic, but personal and focused, approach to our lives, whether at home or in the classroom. Tiny ceremonies can help us develop a conscious use and appreciation of the time we're allotted. Likewise, rituals enable us to be both productive and efficient so we can squeeze the most out of every moment.

MORNING RITUALS

Whether they are intentional or not, we all have morning rituals, activities, and personal ceremonies we perform without a second thought. These rituals probably include hitting the snooze button, showering, eating breakfast, making coffee, and driving to work.

Strong rituals are mindful rituals. Instead of merely being a morning zombie, create short, ten- to twenty-minute rituals that you are actually aware of and, more importantly, mindful while doing.

Suggestions for morning rituals:

- Walk the dog and look at the sky.

- When you bathe or shower, play soft music. Make a conscious effort to feel the soapy foam on your skin and luxuriate in the warm water.

- Meditate for ten minutes.

- Sip your coffee on the front porch or back patio, enjoy the sunrise and listen to the birds.

- Eat breakfast without reading emails or the back of the cereal box. Be one with your Lucky Charms.

- Read something inspirational (poetry, self-help, religious books) for ten minutes.

- Have a meaningful conversation with your child while driving him or her to school.

EVENING RITUALS

Everyone's tired at the end of the day. Parents are spent from a long day at work, and kids are fatigued from school, homework, and frolicking around the neighborhood with their friends. But this universal exhaustion is exactly why it's so important to slow down during the evening and create rituals that will keep you calm, relaxed, and centered.

Suggestions for evening rituals:

- Read to your kids before bed.

- Enjoy bubble baths with incense, candles, and music.

- Read something personally enriching.

- Listen to music.

- Take a walk after dinner.

- Have a glass of wine or a cup of tea and sip it mindfully.

- Have a conversation and spend quality time with your spouse.

- Journal, blog, or write about your life.

- Meditate for ten minutes.

WEEKEND RITUALS

Weekends were intended to be times of rest and relaxation, but Saturday and Sunday have become the default days to accomplish the chores we couldn't quite cram into Monday through Friday. Most religions recommend (even require) a sabbath, or time of rest, for us to recharge our batteries and return to our weekly responsibilities with a replenished sense of vigor. Christianity says that, after putting all of creation into motion, even God rested—so why shouldn't you?

Suggestions for weekend rituals:

- Take a long hike.
- Have brunch at a favorite restaurant.
- Call your parents.
- Enjoy an afternoon gardening.
- Attend church.
- Get together with friends.
- Enjoy breakfast at a local diner—either alone or with friends (one of my absolutely favorite rituals, by the way).

CLASSROOM RITUALS

In the old days, I would arrive at my classroom by 6 a.m., put on coffee, write for forty minutes, and listen to music before my first period students came clambering in at 7:15. It was a deeply fulfilling morning ritual. In short, it was heaven.

But now that my children are older, my responsibilities and schedules have changed. I help out more at home in the mornings. Consequently, I have had to adjust my classroom rituals.

To maintain a fulfilling classroom ritual and balance of work and renewal, I have adopted the following schedule: I work diligently during my prep periods on Mondays, Wednesdays, and Thursdays. On Tuesdays, though, I write during my prep period (since my morning writing time is now gone). And I reserve Fridays for what I call my "Friday Fun Prep." I might have popcorn, sit on a bench outside if the weather's nice, listen to my iPod, catch up on a little Netflix on my cell phone or laptop, meditate at my desk, read something for pleasure, or walk to the nearby park and listen to the birds. I think of it as my classroom sabbath.

You might think my conscience would bother me, and I might feel as if my Friday Fun Preps are stealing from "the man." I just might—if it weren't for the many hours I spend working at home with no monetary compensation whatsoever. So I sleep just fine at night, thank you very much. It's all about balance.

Suggestions for classroom rituals:

- Breathe or meditate before school begins.
- Take a walk around the campus.
- Start each class period with silent reading.
- Start each class period with quiet time.
- Have lunch with a colleague. (I eat with a friend from my department every Wednesday, just for the companionship and camaraderie.)
- Read a bit during free time.
- Write or journal.
- Reflect or plan.
- Collaborate with another teacher about your curriculum.
- Institute a "Genius Hour" or 20% time, during which you focus on a project you're passionate about.
- Steal my Friday Fun Prep idea. (I don't mind!)

Rituals slow down our day and make us present and conscious for at least a small part of each day, every day. And if you choose to be present while your personal ceremonies unfold, even the most ordinary of days will have depth and meaning.

Candles, incense, and sitar music are optional.

ZEN TEACHER ASSIGNMENT

Pick one of the suggestions mentioned in this chapter (morning, evening, weekend, or classroom) and create activities that can become rituals in your life. When you feel those are in place, practice a second one. And then a third. Not only will you feel more focused and organized, but you should find yourself with a surplus of energy that you can expend on your other passions and desires.

SPACE,
STILLNESS,
and
SELF-CARE

Space

Our life is frittered away by detail. . .
Simplify! Simplify! Simplify!
. . . Simplicity of life and elevation of purpose!
—*Henry David Thoreau, Walden*

To drive home the importance of creating space in our lives, I initially thought about putting the word *Space* as the name of the chapter and then leaving the rest of the page intentionally blank. But then I figured you had probably spent your hard-earned money on this book and might not appreciate my little stunt. But creating space in our lives—both in terms of our physical environment and our daily schedules—really is *that* important.

We all have responsibilities and obligations. We all endure times when there is just too much to do, and we spend the day rushing from one appointment to another. In those times, space comes at a premium, if it comes at all.

The problem is that, when every box in our calendar is filled in, every moment is accounted for, every room has clutter, and our lives are hyper-organized, unscheduled obstacles cause great conflict because we do not have the wiggle room we need as a result of scheduling ourselves into a corner. But if we give ourselves permission to create physical and mental space, to give ourselves some breathing room, it suddenly becomes easier to navigate the bumpy parts of our journey and adjust to life's surprises.

When we create space, we are also giving ourselves room to:

- Move smoothly.
- Think profoundly.
- Dream luxuriously.
- Reflect quietly.
- Celebrate spontaneously.
- Mourn deeply.
- Shift direction nimbly.
- Proceed confidently.
- Retreat knowingly.
- Explore spiritually.
- Share generously.
- Dance unashamedly.

If you were to eliminate even one weekly activity or clear off one surface each weekend, how much more space, physically and mentally, would you have? Could you take a two-month hiatus from your book club and then spend that time considering whether or not you really want to return? Could you spend a Saturday afternoon thinning out the bookcase in the family room? Or maybe going through your closet?

When you declutter your life, your spirit feels lighter and your entire world becomes more open and expansive, releasing you from the anxious funk of overwhelming clutter and the oppressive burden of obligation and excess.

The same applies in our classrooms. Our professional lives would benefit from having a little more space, as would our curriculum, our classrooms, and our students. Is there an old, not-so-successful unit you could toss to allow more time and space for your passion project? Be brutal. Be merciless. Is there a way to lose a bookcase, a table, an extra desk, or even a poster on the wall?

Furthermore, I personally promise you that you are still a committed teacher and decent human being if you gracefully bow out of that committee you never really wanted to join in the first place. I repeat: *You're still a committed teacher and decent human being without that obligation.* And if anyone says differently, give that person my number; we'll talk.

But there's a catch: No one is going to give you space.

Space is a choice. And the choice is up to you.

First, you must value it. And then you must insist on it.

But if you do, you will soon see that choosing space is an invaluable gift to yourself and a meaningful step toward your inherent right to self-care.

ZEN TEACHER ASSIGNMENT

Start small. Set an intention in your life for where you'd like a little more space—in the home, the classroom, on your calendar, with your obligations, or with the people you know. Even recognizing where you'd like the space to occur is a great first step to making it happen.

Subtraction

As teachers, we want to make a difference.

We also want to stick around for a while, so we often make overt attempts to display the breadth of our skills and prove that we can be team players. We take on every project, grant every request, and agree to every opportunity.

I know because I did it, too.

Teaching jobs were scarce in 1993, and I wanted to show how great a teacher I was because, quite frankly, I needed a job. So while still a temporary employee, I directed the school play, contributed articles to the staff newsletter, and was the PTSA teacher representative. I even coached the teacher team in the faculty/senior basketball game. That level of commitment might have made sense at the time, but I've since learned that trying to be a master of all things puts you on the A-train directly to Burnout Land. The irony is, the more junk and clutter we have in our lives, the worse we teach.

Enter subtraction.

Nike CEO Mark Parker says Apple visionary Steve Jobs told him that focus "means saying no to the hundred other good ideas that there are."

Two decades into my career, I'm finally making a conscious effort to rid my teaching life of excess. Case in point: a large bookcase filled with my favorite acting, writing, and literature books has stood against a wall in my office for decades, probably since *My Cousin Vinny* was in movie theaters.

I recently noticed, however, that the bookcase was separating at the joints. Looking at the buckling sides, I worried the whole thing would collapse and crush one of my teaching assistants.

When I couldn't find a replacement to fit the space, it dawned on me that the universe was encouraging me to subtract. After removing and finding homes for the most important books, I dismantled the bookcase and tossed its remnants in the dumpster behind the woodshop. I simplified, opened up a significant amount of space in my office, and, as a result, allowed myself to breathe.

What junk are you holding onto for someday?

Maybe you still have your notebooks from when you were studying for your teaching certification exam. Maybe you're just certain that, one day, you will use that excellent worksheet on irony. Maybe you really don't need to keep that license plate from your very first car or your collection of homemade VHS tapes of every episode of *Saved By The Bell*. (Can these even be played anymore?) Similarly, is that coffee mug from the bowling tournament in 1989 doing anything more than just taking up space on the shelf?

If you haven't used something in the past six months, it's unlikely that you'll ever use it again. Ever. If that's true, then the question becomes, why allow it to take up space in your life, home, or classroom?

Subtraction clearly applies to stuff. It can also be practiced on a more philosophical level. Maybe you can subtract the stress of worrying about how your hair looks or what the teacher down the hall thinks of the "mess" in your classroom. Maybe you can subtract the desire to eat fried foods or the need to watch that third episode of *Survivor* on Hulu.

This is not to say you have to live like an ascetic in a one-room hovel with only a cot, folding chair, and washbowl for sponge baths. Rather, subtracting what you don't need, mentally and physically, can create peace, focus, and simplicity in your classroom—and your mind. If you look around and decide your life would benefit from a little laser-focused surgery, ask yourself:

- Where is the excess?
- What can I get rid of?
- What is my focus?
- What will give me a sense of space and breathing room?
- What can I eliminate and still reach my goals?
- What is the most important thing that I want to say happened in my classroom?
- What details are merely filler and make my overall mission cloudy or blur the lines of my purpose?

If you have taught for any length of time, chances are you have accumulated an assortment of materials, supplies, projects, examples, forms, worksheets, and shoeboxes overflowing with various bric-a-brac.

But do you need it all?

Really? All the time?

Probably not.

In my days as a college drama major, I was a total packrat. I kept everything under the pretense that, in my travels as an actor, I might use it someday. I envisioned being cast in a play and, journeyman actor that I was, opening up a trunk and finding the perfect red bowtie, a frayed top hat, a pair of wire-rimmed spectacles—whatever I needed for the role. It seemed wise. It was fun. And it made me feel like a dedicated actor. But mostly, it filled my apartment with a bunch of useless junk. What junk are you holding onto for someday? The reality is, just like me and my collection of costumes and props, it's unlikely that you will ever even think about (let alone, use) the materials you've stashed away.

In the *New York Times'* bestseller *Steal Like an Artist*, artist and writer Austin Kleon shares a blackout poem he wrote that says simply, "Creativity is subtraction."

And he's right. Sometimes what we choose to eliminate can have as profound an influence as what we include. What we choose to leave out can create room for our art and our passion, and make space for us so that our life can soar. To choose more in our lives, therefore, we must often start by choosing less.

ZEN TEACHER ASSIGNMENT

Evaluate your life: scheduled events, hobbies, responsibilities, obligations, and even people. Then pick one or two things you can do without and create space by subtracting them from the equation of your life.

Decluttering

What if I told you that I have a method that will give you more time to pursue your passions, your priorities, and your pet projects? What if I told you it could help ease your tension and eliminate much of your stress? And what if I said that this magic method is less about adding something new to your already overscheduled life and more about taking something away?

Would you be interested?

The key to attaining all these benefits may surprise you: it's decluttering.

Every new year, many of us set decluttering as a goal, fire ourselves up, take a frantic and scattered run at it, burn out, and give up. Afterward, we throw our hands in the air and say, "See? I knew that wouldn't work!"

But decluttering isn't simply about removing all the random, useless stuff from our lives, although that's part of it. We've already looked at a few reasons subtraction is important, but it's also important to know how the clutter got there in the first place so that you can prevent new clutter from crowding your freshly cleared spaces.

HOW CLUTTER ACCUMULATES

The cancer at the core of the clutter problem is our society's lust for "stuff." We are conditioned from a very early age to believe that the more we have, the happier we will be. I spent years on this treadmill, knowing that less might be better, and yet it took a very long time for me to have the courage to change.

You may be in a similar place, and that's okay. Think of decluttering as a process with starts and stops and stumbles along the way. But if you are stumbling toward your ultimate goal, then it's all good.

Teachers keep all sorts of random things "just in case." "Just in case I need it for a lesson." "Just in case I ever do that unit again." "Just in case computer punch cards come back or I want to play my Steppenwolf eight-track tapes again." (Believe me, I'm making fun of me, not you. I did this for years.)

No more.

My classroom is far from perfectly decluttered, but it is leaps and bounds ahead of where it was, and I have the rest of my career to perfect it. As *Zen Habits* blogger Leo Babauta says, "Clutter didn't create itself. It's there because you put it there."

So the question becomes, "Why did I put it there?"

If I don't have a good answer, out it goes.

HOW TO DECLUTTER YOUR CLASSROOM

The following is not an exhaustive list of ways to declutter, but it should go a long way toward helping you remove the unnecessary from your life and classroom:

1. ***Start now.*** You could wait until that "perfect" time, but I promise you it will never come. You could wait until this weekend, the middle of summer, or next fall. Or you could start right now and have a slightly less cluttered classroom by this time tomorrow. It's your call.

2. ***Think small.*** You can spend a weekend emptying your room and piling all of your useless junk in the hallway for the custodian to haul away, but you don't have to. Pick one small area in your classroom and start there.

3. ***Allot fifteen minutes a day.*** And if you don't have fifteen minutes, start with five. You may not think you can make a difference in five minutes but, over time, I guarantee that your space will experience a profound transformation.

4. ***Choose a single surface.*** Sometimes it's enough just to start the day with a clean desk. Even small steps can pay huge dividends when it comes to creating a clean, clear, and positive composition in your classroom environment. Start with an individual shelf, counter, or drawer.

5. **Save first.** Put what you want to save in one pile and then create two other piles marked "give away" and "throw away." I did not invent this idea, but it's a good one and it works!

6. **Handle everything only once.** Make sure everything gets into one of your three piles—the first time. If you need to ease into decluttering, you have my permission to create a "maybe" pile. Just remember to go back to the "maybe" pile and sort everything in it into one of the other three piles.

7. **Give everything a home.** I'm sure this is not the first time you've heard this idea, but how often do you follow it? Be ruthless! Does it go in a drawer, cupboard, or wastebasket? It's your choice, of course, but choose already!

8. **Ignore excuses.** "But I won that stuffed bear at the carnival!" "That necklace came from my eighth-grade boyfriend!" "My grandmother gave me that .357 Magnum!" Actually, you probably shouldn't be keeping that last one in your classroom, but you get my drift.

9. **When something comes, something goes.** When I get something new, I force myself to get rid of something old. Not only does this practice honor the idea that space is finite, but it makes decluttering an ongoing process. You want to avoid finding yourself buried beneath a brand-spanking new pile of more useless junk in a year. Some experts say, "One in, two out," but then I'm all like, "Whoa, slow down, Turbo!"

10. **Celebrate.** Once you have decluttered an area in your classroom, celebrate your success and progress. Take an extra-long break. Have an extra cookie. Buy a yacht. It doesn't really matter what you do, as long as you give yourself permission to accept that you've won a tiny victory and use that celebration to motivate you to keep going.

Once you declutter, you will have the beautiful chore of deciding what to do with all of your extra time, space, energy, and freedom.

ZEN TEACHER ASSIGNMENT

Choose one space in your life—whether it's in your home, car, classroom, or other living area—and spend fifteen minutes decluttering it. In the beginning, the space you choose cannot and should not be large. You do not want to feel overwhelmed, but, instead, motivated by the thrill of success inherent in having decluttered that particular space. Once you have a rhythm down, you can expand both the physical area and the time spent on your decluttering efforts.

Stillness

Learning how to be still,
to really be still and let life happen —
that stillness becomes a radiance.

—*Morgan Freeman*

T**he world is a busy place.** We spend our days and nights consumed by the responsibilities of our jobs, our families, our spouses, our churches, our houses, even our hobbies. There's always something that has to be done. Most of the people I know tell me that they never have time to slow down (let alone stop), never have time to take a moment, never have time to reflect or enjoy or appreciate their lives.

Yet, in the unprecedented increase in activity and busyness in our recent history, there has never been a greater need for finding the time to slow down and practice a little self-care.

You may not have a full day to do what you want to do right now. That's understandable. Much of our lives are spoken for. I get that. You may not even have an hour. Sixty minutes can be a long time to set aside just for yourself.

So how much time can you set aside for yourself? Carving out a little time, even thirty minutes—no longer than the length of the average sitcom—can seem impossible. But I'm going to go out on a limb here and say that everyone has five minutes to spare every day. Everyone. Every single one of us can carve out a measly 300 seconds out of our 86,400 seconds in a day, and clutch them to our overworked, shaking bodies so that we can slow down just a bit.

You could be the busiest person on the face of the planet. You could be living the life of a rock star, flying in a Learjet to London for your next concert, doing back-to-back interviews, dressing in disguise to avoid groupies, doing a sound check and a radio show and a meet-and-greet with a local contest winner, and you could still set aside five minutes. That's the time it takes to yell at the tour manager because your concert rider said yellow M&M's and Pepsi and all you have are green M&M's and Sprite. You have five minutes.

And once you find those five minutes, stop.

And be still.

And look around.

And meditate.

And breathe.

You can listen to a soothing song.

You can read a poem.

You can pray.

Whatever you do, find an activity that means something to you, something that, in those few moments, will bring you back to the present moment, that will allow you to notice what's going on and give you the freedom to reflect on your life, the world, and your spiritual well-being.

I usually spend my five minutes each day listening to music. Most of the classic rock songs I love so much are almost exactly three and a half minutes, but even a long song is only about four minutes or so. No matter how busy I am, I can find time to listen to a single song. (Unless it is Lynyrd Skynyrd's "Free Bird," whose live version clocks in at fourteen minutes.)

We have all been told at some point to "stop and smell the roses." But like all clichés, it's a cliché because in it lies a grain of truth and wisdom.

In this case, there are two: First, you must learn to take time to stop. And second, you must participate in an enjoyable activity that rejuvenates you, brings you back to the present moment, and emphasizes the beauty in the world.

When you start claiming 300 seconds in your day as your own—not your students', not your family's, and not your to-do list's—you'll start relaxing more, and, miraculously, those five minutes will actually become part of your permanent schedule.

And in our hyper-speed, twenty-first-century society, taking time out for ourselves has become a commodity. But when we slow down and take five minutes to reflect on and enjoy and appreciate the world around us, the other 1,435 minutes in our day can't help but benefit.

ZEN TEACHER ASSIGNMENT

Of all of the concepts mentioned in this book, stillness might possibly be the one with which we are most unfamiliar, given the current pace of our society. Nevertheless, it's possible. Take a few moments— as soon as you get up in the morning or right before you go to bed at night—and create an intention to be still. Just sit there. Say nothing. At first, it will drive you crazy. With practice, you will probably find stillness becoming a more common part of your life. It may even become as addicting as our society's unyielding rush to keep moving.

Silence

Silence is a forgotten art. Accustomed to the cacophony of the modern world, many people are uneasy with silence. When there is no sound, our mind calms down, and we are forced to confront the reality of our situation, and that's not always pretty. But spending time in silence can also be an incredibly rich, relaxing, and life-affirming experience—for something that freaks us out, that is. It's only when everything is still that we can sync ourselves to the underlying meter and rhythm of the rest of the universe.

Quaker philosopher William Penn said, "True silence is the rest of the mind and is to the spirit what sleep is to the body, nourishment and refreshment."

If we change our approach to silence as Penn describes, it becomes a refreshing, rejuvenating resource that can help us center ourselves, tune into our deeper thoughts and feelings, and reduce stress and tension. The interference of the outside world melts away, and we are more receptive to simplicity and peace, ideas and solutions, reflection and prayer, nature, and God.

Be intentional about inviting silence into your life every single day.

It's simple enough to create pockets of silence in your day. Take time during the school day to sit in a quiet classroom. Take a walk in the evening and enjoy some silence among nature. Park your car a few blocks from home and take a few quiet moments for yourself before re-entering the hubbub of family life.

Be intentional about inviting silence into your life every single day.

ZEN TEACHER ASSIGNMENT

Carve out ten minutes today and spend it entirely in silence. Lie on your bed, go to the park, take a walk, relax on the patio, or sit in your car. Embrace whatever ambient noise you hear, but make none of your own. After the ten minutes has passed, reflect on your experience and consider the benefits of spending time each day appreciating silence.

Serenity

This week has been tough. My car has been in the shop for five days, and the ongoing cost of the rental car continues to *cha-ching* itself all over my brain. One of our dogs was extremely ill, so we had to make some hard choices about her treatment. To top it off, the rest of my family spent the week prepping for a trip to attend a wedding in San Francisco, while I stayed behind to continue working my magic in the classroom. It's been stressful, to say the least.

I needed some peace and quiet. Some calm. Some serenity.

Serenity is the quality of being calm, peaceful, tranquil, and untroubled. While it's unrealistic to expect to maintain a state of serenity all of the time, we see the value in pursuing such a state when we are privileged enough to experience a moment or two of serenity in our own lives. Every profession has its stressors and pressures, but when it comes to teaching, experiencing serenity can ultimately improve not only your health and your mindset but also your teaching practice.

How I seek my moments of serenity varies, but it usually depends on what kind of time I have. Looking for a moment of peace and harmony can be as simple as taking a few slow, closed-eyed breaths between classes. Or it might be a matter of sitting in a dark room and meditating, reflecting, or praying. Sometimes I recapture a sense of calm by putting in my earbuds and listening to some classic rock on my iPod, eyes closed, mind wandering. Like my father, I have often found moments of intense peace while listening to Joe Cocker, Creedence Clearwater Revival, Rod Stewart, The Beatles, and The Rolling Stones. Regaining your center by leaning back in a recliner and listening to "Lookin' Out My Back Door" or "Long As I Can See the Light" is not a bad way to go.

However, if I have more time, my approach is grander.

I am a card-carrying believer in "mental health" days (when exercised judiciously), so yesterday I played hooky from school. I arranged for a sub the night before, wrote some lesson plans, and was ready to rock.

My first rule for mental health days is no alarm, so I woke up when I woke up. After feeding the animals, I took a long, slow shower. One of my favorite things to do is to have breakfast in a diner, and so I did just that: two eggs over medium, extra-crispy hash browns, sourdough toast with grape jelly, and finally (and perhaps most importantly), hot, black coffee.

Pursuing serenity, both inside and outside the classroom, should always be a priority for a Zen Teacher.

In San Diego, there is a place near downtown called Seaport Village. It is a collection of upscale shops and boutiques that edge up next to the bay. From its meandering paths, you can see a wide expanse of the Pacific Ocean, majestic gray Navy ships, and small sailboats inching along. On the other side of the bay, you can also see the swaying palm trees and stately mansions of Coronado Island. I'm convinced this paradise was designed expressly to give both tourists and locals alike a portal back to their own sense of serenity.

After strolling the boardwalk, greeting the caricaturist and tarot card readers, perusing the newest volumes in the coffeehouse/bookstore, spending some quality quiet time in the art gallery, and stepping into a few boutiques, I ended up on a bench near one of the shops that faces the water. For almost two decades now, I have thought of this spot as "my" bench. And what do I do while sitting on "my" bench?

Absolutely nothing.

Well, actually, that's not entirely true. I smile at the salesmanship of the sunglasses and popcorn vendors. I enjoy watching the seabirds dive for fish. I observe the joggers, families, tourists, and business folks, whose lanyard nametags give them away as conference attendees from the nearby hotels. I listen to the horns on the Navy ships. I chat with the sparrows that are so accustomed to human contact that they congregate on the wood planks at my feet. This mini-retreat is a great opportunity to reflect on my life, think about what I need to stop doing, what I should continue, and what I should change.

Mostly, though, I just look at the water.

Pursuing serenity, both inside and outside the classroom, should always be a priority for a Zen Teacher. When stress hits, finding a way to create serenity can help you recapture a sense of balance, peace, and harmony—in your day-to-day experiences in the classroom and in every other area of your life. When you learn to carve out your own bit of serenity, you will, without a doubt, notice the difference. And so will your students and loved ones.

ZEN TEACHER ASSIGNMENT

Find your happy place. And then go there as often as you can. Pick a happy place in the outside world, as well as one that is in or near your classroom or at your school. One of my favorite happy places is Seaport Village and "my" bench. At my school, there is a bench right outside my classroom where I go when I need to decompress and find a moment of serenity. Where is your happy place? And what's stopping you from going there right now?

Put Down Your Sword

A big, tough samurai once went to see a little monk. "Monk," he said, in a voice that demanded instant obedience, "teach me about heaven and hell!"

The monk looked up at this mighty warrior and replied with utter disdain, "Teach you about heaven and hell? I couldn't teach you anything. You're dirty. You smell. Your blade is rusty. You're a disgrace, an embarrassment to the samurai class. Get out of my sight; I can't stand you."

The samurai was furious. He shook, got all red in the face, and was speechless with rage. He pulled out his sword and raised it above him, preparing to slay the monk.

"That's hell," the monk said softly.

The samurai was overwhelmed. The compassion and surrender of this little man who had offered his life to give this teaching, to show him hell! He slowly put down his sword, filled with gratitude, and suddenly peaceful.

"And that's heaven," said the monk softly.

The theme of this short fable that comes from mindfulness master Jack Kornfield's website is that heaven equates to choosing peace, compassion, and tranquility, and putting down our (metaphorical) swords and rejecting rage, anger, and violence. It resonates with me because it's easy to get caught up in the heat of the moment. In these heated moments, courage is required to keep our wits about us enough to step back and put down our sword.

As Zen Teachers who are constantly seeking peace and tranquility in our classrooms, we must put down our swords to embrace "heaven" and reject "hell," or violence and aggression. And when I say violence, I am not talking about gunfire, fistfights, or even, as in the case of the story, swordplay. Rather, I'm talking about how we hurt ourselves by holding on to and suppressing anger, hostility, bitterness, and resentment. If we can learn to put down our swords, we will feel calmer and more self-possessed.

During a recent reading of Shirley Jackson's "The Lottery," I noticed that a student in the front row had fallen asleep. As I woke him up, the class began laughing, and the student blushed in embarrassment. In an effort to lessen the student's disorientation and confusion from having been woken up, I told a joke. He started laughing, and soon the entire class joined in. Before long, the ominous tone of Jackson's tale of a public human sacrifice had gone out the window.

I could have gotten angry.

But instead, I put down my sword.

I detached from any preconceived expectation of outcome, laughed along with the class, practiced lovingkindness, and accepted the moment for what it was. Mostly, though, I just waited. We didn't have as long or as deep a discussion of the "The Lottery" as the other sophomore classes did that day, but I did create a peaceful atmosphere, retain a good rapport with the class, and teach with a sense of grace. Not bad progress, considering I hadn't even had lunch yet.

I could have chided, admonished, and berated the class, but I've realized that, when someone slights us, more often than not, it is a creation of our own perception, however skewed it may be. And our feelings may be hurt a little, but we can choose to put that aside and put down our sword. In short, we can choose a better response.

A warrior in constant battle
is a tired warrior.
And teachers are tired enough.

- When the driver cuts you off on the highway, put down your sword.
- When a student pushes your last button, put down your sword.
- When a colleague takes credit for your idea, put down your sword.
- When that kid in seventh period disrupts your lesson for the third time, write a referral. And then put down your sword.

I'm not suggesting we let others take advantage of us or that we never stand up and fight for what we believe in. You know yourself best, and you will have to determine when it is in your best interest to fight the battle and when it is better to let things go.

But I can tell you this:

A warrior in constant battle is a tired warrior.

And teachers are tired enough.

Zen Teacher Assignment

Be mindful of one experience that is frustrating you, angering you, or annoying you. Next, with a complete sense of non-judgment and detachment, put down your sword. And then move on, leaving the frustration, anger, or annoyance on the ground with your dropped weapon.

Yield and Overcome

Imagine a spindly, bare tree branch enduring a harsh winter snow-storm. After a while, the snow piles up on the branch, adding extra weight and pressure. If the branch is stiff and unbending, it will eventually break. But if the branch is flexible and yields to the burden, it will bend toward the ground, and eventually the snow will slide off and the branch will spring back, unhurt.

The bending branch can teach us a thing or two.

In the *Tao Te Ching*, a centuries-old, classic Chinese guide on living, author and philosopher Lao Tzu writes, "Yield and overcome." It's a simple concept, yet reading it radically affected my attitude toward being flexible and acquiescing to others. That's because where I once thought yielding signaled weakness and giving in, the *Tao Te Ching* teaches us that it actually requires strength to bend, to be so flexible that you can allow burdens to glide right off you. We yield and overcome not because we are pushovers, but because we are refusing to get caught up in the insignificant battles directly in front of us. We are pursuing alternate (and more valuable) priorities based on a larger vision. Yield and overcome is about giving the universe a giant "Whatever!" and saying, "Talk to the hand because I deserve better than this."

For Zen Teachers, the concept of yield and overcome has many practical applications, including helping you to save your energy and sanity. With this mindset of bending when possible, you can choose your battles wisely, release what isn't really important, and reduce the drama in your life. And who couldn't do with a little less drama?

Here are three ways to yield and overcome.

CHOOSE YOUR BATTLES

You don't have to engage in every conflict that comes along. If another teacher slights you in the duplication room, if an administrator treats you unfairly, if a student doesn't understand the beauty of your lesson, shake it off. Yield and bend. Do the biblical turn-the-other-cheek thing. The immediate injustice might be a bitter pill at first. But if you pay attention, you will notice that yielding to a greater motive will increase your personal joy.

YOU DON'T ALWAYS HAVE TO BE RIGHT

Always being right requires a tremendous amount of energy, and it is a huge waste of time. Taking a stand, digging in your heels, and refusing to budge from your position are exhausting and only create strife. By the end of the conversation, everybody's tired and there are no real winners. Unless the issue at hand really matters long-term, let the other person be right. Your energy is better spent elsewhere, like reaching and fulfilling your potential.

WALK AWAY

If you hear rumors, innuendo, or gossip, you can either choose to be a part of it or you can walk away. Let me give you a tip: Drama isn't worth your time, energy, or emotions. Nor does it help you be a better or more effective teacher, parent, spouse, or friend.

By yielding, you most definitely overcome. You will gain:

- More time
- More energy
- A clearer focus
- More goals achieved
- More potential reached
- A stronger sense of self

Be willing to bend. Reap the benefits of letting a little snow slide from your branch.

ZEN TEACHER ASSIGNMENT

During the next school day, when you encounter a situation that is causing anger, frustration, or annoyance, take a moment and remember to let the snow slide from the branch. Deciding to yield is up to you. And once you yield, the overcoming part will just be the universe's gift to you.

Non-Doing

It is tempting to look at someone doing nothing and call them a loafer, a couch potato, a goof-off. But doing nothing is not necessarily laziness. "Non-doing" actually requires making a conscious decision to resist always being on the go, to always being active.

Part of non-doing involves non-judgment. As mindfulness meditation expert Jon Kabat-Zinn advises, "Work at allowing more things to unfold in your life without forcing them to happen and without rejecting the ones that don't fit your idea of what 'should' be happening."

Yes, we may have a thousand obligations and a million things on our to-do list, but it's important, even in the midst of all of that, to stop and experience some non-doing without judging, criticizing, or punishing ourselves for laziness. Rather, we should spend time letting the world do what the world wants to do. And as indispensable as we feel, I promise you, life can do without us for a few minutes. And if you feel pressured by others to do something, it may help you to remember this saying: "If you ask me what I'm doing and I say, 'Nothing,' that doesn't mean I'm free. That means I'm doing nothing."

You have the right, of course, to do whatever you want with your leisure time, and that may include playing sports or games. But I'd like to encourage you not to always spend your downtime participating in mindless activities and busyness or active, energetic, overscheduled "fun" because, when you return from that "relaxation," you will still feel tense and uptight.

So if you can't do while you're non-doing, how, exactly, do you non-do? It might look something like:

- Taking a walk in silence.
- Sitting and meditating.
- Lying on your bed and breathing.

- Sitting on your patio, doing nothing but listening to the birds and watching the clouds.
- Closing your door when your students go to recess and just sitting at your desk with your eyes closed.
- Sitting quietly for a few minutes when you first rise in the morning or before you go to bed at night (or both).
- Watching a sunrise or a sunset.
- Sitting on the couch for five minutes without talking or making any noise at all.
- Looking at the mountains.
- Parking by the side of the road on your way home from school and sitting for ten minutes.
- Watching your pets.
- Watching your children.

In non-doing, we operate from a place of trust, rather than fear. We trust, first, that non-doing is an acceptable practice. We trust that everything will get done. And we trust that the universe is doing what it's supposed to and that everything is in harmony.

The average teaching day can be so hectic and chaotic that I try to find some time every day to practice non-doing in my classroom. Whether it's before school, during our fifteen-minute break, at lunch, on my prep period, or after school, I look for opportunities to sit and let the world do what it needs to around me, while I simply sit and breathe. Not only has this time become wonderfully restorative for me personally, but it has also enhanced my overall teaching experience.

With practice, non-doing can relax us, renew us, and re-focus us. It can reduce our stress, tension, and anxiety. So the next time you ask yourself, "What should I do now?" consider telling yourself, "Nothing, absolutely nothing."

ZEN TEACHER ASSIGNMENT

Take five minutes. Don't *do*.
Really, I mean it. Tell them I said it was okay.

Where's the Fire?

In the last twenty years, I have gotten married, had kids, taken on a mortgage, and hit my stride in the classroom. In addition to the numerous gifts these new life experiences have offered, I've also found myself living with an amped-up personal rhythm as well as a truckload of responsibilities, all of which seemingly need to be taken care of right now. These last twenty years have been a whirlwind of excitement, to be sure, but they have also been exhausting and stressful.

At one point, my personal merry-go-round was spinning so fast, I felt as if someone had jerked the crank all the way to the *Holy crap! Hold on for dear life!* setting, and I was about to be sent rocketing into space.

Something needed to change. I needed off the merry-go-round. So I began focusing on living a more present, mindful life and discovered a life truth that has made me happier than I've been in years. I call it "Where's the Fire?"

I realized that I was tired of hurrying, tired of rushing through activities because there was always something else that needed to happen in the next few minutes. My family's schedule made every activity—good or bad, work or pleasure, desire or chore—seem rushed, hastened, and merely something to cross off a list. I rarely had time to stop and enjoy, and certainly not to experience, each of these activities.

Despite your best efforts, responsibilities and obligations will sometimes line up in a way that prevents you from slowing and being present. And that's okay—sometimes. Even I catch myself getting too busy now and then. When that happens, Billy Joel's song "Vienna" comes to mind:

Where's the fire, what's the hurry about?
You better cool it off before you burn it out.
You got so much to do and only
So many hours in a day.

I have found the key to slowing down is structuring your schedule so that, no matter what obligations you have, you have margin—pockets of time without anything scheduled—surrounding that task so you can focus on it without feeling like you have to hurry up and be done because you have somewhere to be or something else to do.

Nowhere is scheduling margin more important than in our class-rooms. We worry about covering the entirety of the state-mandated cur-riculum, and, if a group of students needs extra help or a district assess-ment is suddenly tossed into the mix, we can feel even more behind. We take short breaths, our mind scatters, and our stress level shoots through the roof.

And yet no one but you can change how you schedule your time. You are the boss of your own life, your own calendar, and, of course, your own classroom. If you want things to change, you must take responsibil-ity for changing them.

I want you to try an experiment. Set aside one day next week where you don't have to rush. Pick one concept or topic you want to cover and then give yourself the time you need to focus solely on that concept. Then bask in the margin you've created on both sides of that concept or activity. Create in yourself, your classroom environment, and your stu-dents the sense that there's nowhere else you have to be but here, dealing with that concept at that moment.

No one but you can change how you schedule your time.

Your students may waste time. Let them. You will find that there are still others in the little desks who, like you, will recognize and wel-come the opportunity to take a breath and really dig into the material because they aren't feeling the need to rush. Learning—real learning, that is—happens in the gaps where students think, reflect, and take their time. But that can't happen if we're constantly saying, "C'mon, hurry up! Finish that worksheet. Finish that poster. Are you done with that graphic organizer yet? Remember, *To Kill a Mockingbird* in three minutes!"

At this point, you may be asking, "But what if I don't get to everything?"

I don't know what will happen if you don't cover every word of the prescribed curriculum, but I can tell you what won't happen. The world won't collapse, communism won't be a threat, and other countries won't beat us on standardized testing. Or maybe they will, but who cares? (Whew, that sure felt good!) The bottom line is, if you present even one concept to your students as if it's the only thing of real importance in that moment, you radically increase the chance for deeper, more meaningful learning that will linger in both of your memories much longer than a rushed lesson ever could. And in my book (and as luck would have it, this is my book), that's worth the risk.

Ask yourself, "What would happen if deeper learning occurred because there was space and time? What if, as a bonus, it led to more peace and tranquility in my classroom, in my heart, and in hearts of my students?"

It's easy to think that we have to get to this thing, that thing, or the third thing, but even if we don't, the river of life will usually continue to flow, and we'll all survive. But if we take our time getting there, if we refuse to rush through our teaching and learning, we may survive with just a bit more happiness and peace in our hearts.

ZEN TEACHER ASSIGNMENT

Choose one task you have to do today and build a time and space buffer around it, so that you don't feel rushed or anxious about its completion. And then send out an intention to make that task a mindful experience—whether it's doing a load of laundry, getting your oil changed, or teaching a lesson on figure drawing in your art class. Whatever it is, just allow it to take as long as it takes.

Idleness

Sometimes I ask the students I tutor a very important question: "What did you do last week for fun?"

Without exception, they stare at me with glazed eyes and mumble for a few moments until, out of a heartbreaking sense of pity, I let them off the hook. Parents who are able and willing to pay a credentialed teacher to come into their home to give their child extra help are, almost exclusively, not doing this because their child is failing or lacks skills. The parents hire a tutor because they want their child to not simply do well, but to excel.

There's nothing wrong with high expectations, a strong work ethic, or superior achievement. But these students' lives are so crammed with violin and tennis lessons, SAT and ACT preparation classes, and debate and soccer tournaments that they are stumped for an answer when someone asks them what they do just for fun. Some of these activities may, in fact, be enjoyable, but after digging deeper, I often learn that they are involved with these activities not because it's fun or because it's their passion. They participate in them because, "My mom and dad made me" or because, "Everyone else is doing it" or, most frighteningly, because, "It looks good on a college application."

Our students have, by and large, forgotten the fine art of just hanging out. This is a problem. Overscheduled children are kept so busy that they don't learn how to entertain themselves. They don't know how to play without the aid of others or a video game. It turns out that this constant stimulation inhibits their imagination and creativity. As they grow older, the continual and urgent need to "do" will become an impediment, damaging their spirit and crippling their productivity.

I remember when my friends and I would ride our bikes around my neighborhood (in my nerdy, eight-year-old mind, I called them my "bike tours"), hang out in canyons, climb the hill above my house, and not come home until the streetlights came on or we heard our mothers calling our names from our front porches. There was no plan, no play-dates, no structure, no overriding goal. We just did whatever occurred to us in the moment.

That kind of freedom and wild abandon may not be possible any-more. And yet I mourn for the loss of that unstructured time for today's teenagers. Mostly I mourn because they don't even know what they're missing.

I recently told one boy who seemed particularly unsure of what I meant by "having fun" and "goofing off" that I was going to give him some homework. He readied his pen. I told him he wouldn't need to take notes but that I was going to suggest something that was probably going to freak him out. Then he looked really nervous. "Some time during the coming week," I said, "I want you to take twenty minutes and do absolutely nothing. Sit under a tree and look at the sky. Or go to the mall, get a soda, sit on a bench, and just watch people. Or just lie on your bed and stare at the ceiling." Judging from the appalled look on his face, you would have thought I asked him to shank his sister with a rusty screwdriver.

Sadly, this issue isn't restricted to young people. Adults also schedule themselves silly. In an article in the *New York Times* titled "The Busy Trap," Tim Kreider explains that the average person is not only "crazy-busy" as a result of his own choices, but that this busyness also has a rather dark origin. "Busyness," he writes, "serves as a kind of existential reassurance, a hedge against emptiness; obviously your life cannot possibly be silly or trivial or meaningless if you are so busy, completely booked, in demand every hour of the day."

Kreider's claim implies that, as grownups, we use the crutch of keep-ing busy to increase our self-esteem and sense of security to justify our existence, to stave off loneliness and the possible "nightmare" of finding ourselves alone with nothing to do, no goal, no anticipated outcome. Everything about our culture tells that we must keep moving, we must keep going, we must keep trying. Stopping, on the other hand, is for laggards, loafers, and do-nothings.

The writer further praises the necessity of non-doing when he says:

Idleness is not just a vacation, an indulgence or a vice; it is as indispensable to the brain as vitamin D is to the body, and, deprived of it, we suffer a mental affliction as disfiguring as rickets. The space and quiet that idleness provides is a necessary condition for standing back from life and seeing it whole, for making unexpected connections and waiting for the wild summer lightning strikes of inspiration—it is, paradoxically, necessary to getting any work done.

The world is spinning so fast that we forget we're supposed to enjoy it.

Goofing off, it seems, is serious business. The time and space (and, most importantly, the ability) to be with ourselves in a largely unstructured block of time and either do whatever we want or, perhaps, do absolutely nothing at all gives us the opportunity for reflection, insight, and skill-building that will benefit us the rest of our lives. It's an opportunity many students don't have these days because of our emphasis on achievement, activity, and business.

The point here is that teachers are no different. The world is spinning so fast that we forget we're supposed to enjoy it.

So this is your reminder.

Starting tonight, I challenge you to do something fun.

Don't be like the students I tutor, who look glassy-eyed when someone asks, "What did you do for fun, just for you?"

You've worked hard.

You've earned it.

And if you're waiting for the science teachers to agree, let me save you the effort: Research has shown that when you engage in idleness, in goofing off, in doing something just because it's fun, you improve your work/life balance, a shift that can result in a greater sense of peace, calm, and equanimity. And if you don't believe science, believe in something more akin to our current social rhythm: fast food. Even McDonald's had a slogan that said, "You deserve a break today."

A month or so ago, I saw my youngest daughter sitting in an easy chair in our office, her eyes reflecting the silver glow of the iPad screen. She is a straight-A student with a wicked sense of humor.

"What are you doing?" I asked.

"Watching videos."

"On YouTube?"

"Yeah."

"So basically, you're just goofing off?" I asked.

Her brow furrowed and she frowned as if she might be in trouble. "Uh, yeah. I guess."

I smiled widely and raised my arm with an open hand. "High-five!" I yelled.

Smiling, she high-fived me.

And then we talked about the importance of downtime.

ZEN TEACHER ASSIGNMENT

I am giving you the same homework I gave my tutoring client: Find twenty minutes in your day or night and just be idle. Do nothing. Sit in a lawn chair in the yard and look at the clouds. Lie on your bed and stare at the ceiling. Walk to the top of the hill behind your house and sit and do nothing. Recharge your batteries through the magic of intentional idleness. It can be transformative.

Self-Care

Love yourself first, and everything else falls in
line. You really have to love yourself
to get anything done in this world.
— *Lucille Ball*

We don't keep driving our cars when the "check engine" light comes on, but as teachers, we have this uncanny ability to ignore the signals that our bodies—those crazy, unpredictable vehicles that drive us through life—send us.

I recently read a teacher's blog in which the writer lamented that he felt he was disappointing his students when he took a sick day. He thought he had let them down by not being there to guide them through a complicated project. It's an argument I often hear—I've even made it myself. I mean, who better to guide your students to the most effective and successful outcome than you?

Great teachers, though, often push themselves too far; they tend to overdo it, ignore their body's signals, and overextend themselves physically, mentally, and emotionally. They forget about this tiny little thing called balance. We're only human, after all, not machines.

We work around young people (and their germs) every single day of our careers. The fact that we don't spend six months a year in an iron lung is a miracle of biblical proportions. So whenever I feel run down or need to take a day off, I try to remember that teaching is a continuum. These children? Yes, they're important. But so are the students you will have next year, the year after that, and in ten years. And if you ignore the signs and signals that your body is giving right now, if you insist on going to school when you're not well, you run the risk of greater health issues down the road. Plus, if you take the time today to renew your health, you will return tomorrow an even better teacher to your current students.

The Zen Teacher pays attention to his or her body and learns the language of its messages. And when it's time to rest, Zen Teachers rest. And when it's time to be well, they call a sub.

Let's take a walk through your body and check the status of your well-being. As we go through the checklist, sense each part of your body and make a mental note of any problem, discomfort, or misalignment. Do not forget to acknowledge, too, when your body is giving you warm, comfortable, or positive feelings. Do your best to notice everything your body is telling you without judgment or expectation. Whenever you feel off-center, uncomfortable, or are hurting, running through this quick physical inventory can help you isolate the problem so you can understand exactly what you're dealing with and decide how to proceed.

BODY

1. **Head.** Does your head feel comfortable on your neck and shoulders? Does it hurt? And if so, where? Temples? Crown? Scalp? Do you feel any discomfort in your eyes, nose, or mouth? Is your jaw relaxed?

2. **Neck.** How is your posture? Are your muscles tense? Does your neck swivel easily, or is there tension, stress, or discomfort?

3. **Shoulders.** Are your shoulders relaxed or knotted with stress? Do they move and sway easily?

4. **Chest.** Is the chest upright? Sunken? Are you breathing easily, or is it labored?

5. **Arms.** Are your arms comfortable at your sides, or do they hang limply, listlessly?

6. **Hands.** Are your hands comfortable and relaxed? Fidgety? Do you know what to do with them and where to put them?

7. **Fingers.** Are your fingers dexterous and nimble? Thick and plodding?

8. **Back.** Is there any discomfort behind your shoulders? In the small of your back?

9. **Abdomen.** Are your muscles tight? Relaxed? Is there any discomfort, pain, or tension?

10. **Pelvis.** If you swivel your hips, does it hurt at all? Can you comfortably bend at the waist?

11. **Knees.** Can you bend over without your knees hurting or cracking? Are the joints relaxed and comfortable?

12. **Ankles.** Do your ankles swivel smoothly? Any discomfort, pain, or tension?

13. **Calves.** Are the muscles in your calves relaxed and at rest? Do they hurt?

14. **Feet.** Do you feel any pain when you walk? In the balls of your feet? When your heels hit the ground? Or are your feet relaxed and comfortable?

15. **Toes.** Do your toes feel smooshed or scrunched up? Should you be wearing more comfortable shoes? Socks? Spending some time barefoot?

OTHER AREAS TO CHECK FOR SIGNS OF ILLNESS

1. **Throat.** Do you feel any pain in your throat? Is it raw or sore?

2. **Stomach.** Do you feel any nausea? Cramping? Tightness?

3. **Eyes.** Are they burning? Watering?

4. *Head.* Do have any head pain? Is it just a run-of-the-mill head-ache? Migraine? Something else altogether?

General Assessment

- Overall, how does your body feel?

- In general, do you feel as if you are coming down with anything? (An obvious question, but you'd be surprised how many people simply ignore these signs. So it helps to stop and ask.)

- After the inventory, do you notice any stress, tension, or discomfort?

- Does any part of your body still need any stretching or massaging to feel more comfortable or relaxed?

- Would your body benefit from a moment or two of deep breathing or meditation?

It's important that our bodies are comfortable, relaxed, and healthy—for longevity, for ease of living, even for happiness. Because in the end, it's all connected: Body. Mind. Heart. Spirit. If one is out of whack, then all of it is. As Buddha said, "To keep the body in good health is a duty... otherwise we shall not be able to keep our mind strong and clear."

ZEN TEACHER ASSIGNMENT

Take a moment and do a physical inventory of your body. Once you have run through the inventory and checked the status of each part of your body, listen to the signals and address any issues you find through rest, diet, or seeking medical help, if necessary.

Just Say No

In 1982, the United States was introduced to "Just say no," the slogan by Nancy Reagan's anti-drug campaign. Despite the jokes that have been made at the tagline's expense and what some people consider its overly-simplistic answer to the complexities of drug abuse, the First Lady was on to something.

Saying no can be a powerful weapon when it comes to guarding ourselves against substances that can harm us.

But saying no can also guard against other addictions that plague our society—our addiction to speed (as in pacing, not methamphetamines), to overscheduling ourselves and our children, to stuff, to more devices and more screen time, and our all-consuming addiction to louder, faster, and more, more, more.

What can we do about it?

We can just say no.

It's far from easy. Like any addiction, our habits and behaviors are deeply ingrained and must be fought. We are bombarded by the pressure to conform to the group mentality that says these addictions are desirable if we want to fit in, be like the others, and have what others have. But, ultimately, these addictions are a choice.

In our case, deciding to say no to excess possessions, activities, or responsibilities can actually improve the quality of our lives because it gives us the opportunity to pursue the life-enriching behaviors we previously didn't have time for. Saying no does not make you a bad teacher, friend, or person. It is actually the opposite; saying no shows people that you value your personal time and energy, that you respect requests, and that you're actually honoring them by wanting to do the best you can.

Sadly, we assign ourselves more to do simply out of habit, fearing the silence or the stillness of being alone with nothing on our agenda. Simplifying our lives by saying no to the extraneous takes constant vigilance and practice, but the dividends it pays—lower stress levels, a sense of peace, and a clearer perspective on life—are invaluable.

Jon Kabat-Zinn writes in his book, *Wherever You Go, There You Are*, "I practice keeping my life simple, and I find I never do it enough. It's an arduous discipline all its own, and well worth the effort. Yet it is also tricky. There are needs and opportunities to which one must respond."

Despite what society, your spouse, your school, or your administration says, you are under no obligation to accept every opportunity with which you are presented. As the old saying goes, "Just because someone throws you a ball, doesn't mean you have to catch it."

How might your life feel different if you decided to go to just one place less in an afternoon, buy one less item at the store, commit to one less bake sale or car wash or gift wrap sale, or sit on one fewer leadership committee this year? It's not that the bake sale and car wash aren't important (because they are), but you do not have to attend every event. Pace yourself. You will not be a slacker parent. In fact, the extra energy, time, and space you create can be spent on your children in infinitely more fulfilling ways than baking yet another red velvet cupcake.

Saving our time and energy in our classrooms for the truly important can benefit ourselves and our students in many ways. Earlier this year, for example, the vice principal called me into his office and asked me to be involved in something our school calls "Unity Day," when all of our sophomores participate in team-building and bonding exercises. I politely declined his request because:

- I had already participated in that event at least twice.
- I knew that, at that particular moment in time, it would hurt my effectiveness as a classroom teacher.

You are under no obligation to accept every opportunity with which you are presented.

- I was overextended in my personal life, and this activity would take time, energy, and resources I didn't have.
- I was tired, and knew I wouldn't be able to do my best.

After I told him no, the vice principal looked at me and said, "Okay, no problem. Maybe next year." When you say no, you are free to relax, develop a new hobby, or dive into (and focus on) projects and people that are important to you. Here are some suggestions that can improve the quality of your life both at home and in the classroom:

- Take a walk.
- Look at the sky.
- Write that new vocabulary unit.
- Read.
- Spend time with your spouse or children.
- Do a mundane chore like laundry or housecleaning, but without the feeling of being rushed or feeling like you have to be somewhere else.
- Sit in your classroom, look around, and just take a moment to enjoy the learning environment you've created for your lucky students, knowing that their teacher is now less overwhelmed and less stressed.

Saying no is a rebellious act that may ruffle some feathers. Be ready for those reactions and learn to embrace them. But remember that, by learning to simplify and say no, you're giving everyone else a chance to learn from your example. If you give it a chance, saying no can simplify your life in ways you never thought possible. You will be going against the grain of what society expects, but that doesn't make you a victim or a loser.

It just makes you a rebel with the courage to follow your own personal vision.

And that's kinda hot.

ZEN TEACHER ASSIGNMENT

Find an opportunity in your school life to use, as writer Anne Lamott puts it (and as I explain in the next and final chapter), "No as a complete sentence." Watch how it frees up time and space in your life and how that increased time and space adds to your sense of tranquility.

Taking Care of You

If you've ever been on a plane, you've heard the speech that flight attendants give about where the emergency exits are, how to properly secure seat belts, and how the seat cushions double as flotation devices in the event of a water landing.

Crash landings aside, what the flight attendants say about how to use the oxygen masks is a great metaphor for life. In the event of an air emergency, parents are told to put on their masks before placing masks on their children. Look at the mothers on the plane, and you will see them smile quaintly at the thought of putting themselves before their children, but know they are privately thinking, "If those masks drop, you're insane if you think I'm putting my mask on first." Although I'm the first to admit that mothers rock, this children-first, me-second approach, while well-intentioned, can be a bit misguided.

We all know those people who are constantly on the move, always doing something, always feeling like there's more to accomplish. You may even be one of these people. Like mothers who focus on their children's needs before their own, these go-getters never stop to take care of themselves. They rarely, if ever, pause to look around at the world they're so involved in because, "There's just too much to do," or "If I don't do it, who will?" or "People need my help."

If you can relate, you may be at risk of ignoring the needs of your mind, body, and spirit. Giving, serving, and helping is honorable, but failing to practice self-care—to give, serve, and help yourself—comes at a price, both to oneself and to others. You can only operate on "fumes" for so long before putting your health and well-being at risk. Ironically, stopping to refuel and give yourself a little TLC would allow you to produce more, help more, and provide greater quality work.

Writer Anne Lamott introduced me to the term "radical self-care." In her words, radical self-care is when, "I gently bust myself out of the desperate, lifelong need to please, and it means that I start to say no as a complete sentence." It is in the times of anxiety, trouble, and external pressure, Lamott reminds us, that it is most important to remember what exquisite grace there is in loving ourselves and treating ourselves with kindness and compassion.

Value yourself enough to listen to your mind, body, and spirit.

Radical self-care is different for everyone, but it always involves doing something that pampers you, rejuvenates you, supports you, and, most importantly, heals you. Think of it as downtime with a purpose—the purpose being putting yourself back together so you can face the world with a renewed sense of intention and improved vigor.

Radical self-care is:

- Loving yourself for the person you are at this moment and not feeling the need to change to meet anybody else's standard or expectation.

- Valuing yourself enough to listen to your mind, body, and spirit.

- Trusting in who you are and pursuing the person you were meant to be.

Maybe you want to bake cookies or take a bike ride or long walk. Or perhaps today you would rather get a massage or a pedicure. Whatever you choose, find your safety valve—the radical self-care activity that reduces your stress, eases your tension, and renews your spirit—and then do it as often as you can.

Do not ever assume that self-care will just happen on its own. It must be expected, prioritized, and planned for—that's the "radical" part. The world is a roller coaster, and, even though it often doesn't seem like it, only you are in charge of the brakes.

Sure, you may get lucky and find some time here and there to kick back and relax, to catch a game on the tube or—when the sky opens and the cherubs sing—to find yourself stealing a quick nap after Thanksgiving dinner. But those are fortuitous moments that you can't rely on. Yes, those are moments of rest and relaxation, but they are not exactly radical.

Here are some quick tips for implementing radical self-care in your life:

Value it. You have loved ones who care about your well-being and want you to be healthy and mentally sound; however, they may not always have the presence of mind to know what's in your best interests. Besides, they naturally have best interests of their own to protect. Be your own best advocate, and guard your own health and sanity by taking care of yourself.

Schedule it. Remember, your calendar runs everything. If something is on your calendar, it happens. If it's not, well . . . good luck.

Wallow in it. When you reach that moment you've valued and scheduled, enjoy every second of it. This is not the time to worry about the laundry or who will pick up the kids from school—those things will be there when your self-care appointment is over. Let radical self-care be your escape, a way to return to those challenges and obligations with a clearer mind, a ready body, and purer spirit. Be mindful of the opportunity you've been given, and give yourself over to it fully.

Remember it. When you are stressed out or feeling overwhelmed, create a vision of the next time you will be able to give yourself the break you so desperately deserve. When I take my mental health days and go to Seaport Village to sit on "my" bench, for example, I take pictures with the camera on my phone so I can look back when I need it most and remember the calm I felt during those moments. Create a mental picture of your past self-care or the upcoming self-care event that you have planned so you can help yourself find a momentary antidote to your current situation.

It takes courage, passion, and strength to live a life that values radical self-care. As writer and feminist Audre Lorde said, "Caring for myself is not self-indulgence, it is self-preservation, and that is an act of political warfare."

She's right. We cannot expect people to offer us self-care. It is up to us to meet our own needs and provide ourselves with the peace of mind, serenity, and joy that life has to offer.

Think about this: How you would treat someone who was overcome with stress and tension? What would you do? What would you say? What might you give them? My guess is that you would treat them with profound kindness, tenderness, and gentility.

So why, it's worth asking, would you offer yourself anything less?

Zen Teacher Assignment

If I could leave you with any single take-away from this book, it would be this: Give yourself permission to take care of yourself. It's okay. I promise. You deserve to be taken care of by someone you love. And that someone might as well be you.

Conclusion

And so you see I have come to doubt,
all that I once held as true
I stand alone without beliefs,
the only truth I know is You.
— *Paul Simon*

n the Zen tradition, *satori* is the "knowing" that occurs when we finally understand with clarity the truth of some concept with which we have been struggling. It can also be compared to an epiphany or revelation. And so it was that I found my own mini-*satori* when I realized the importance of pursuing a Zen-inspired environment in my classroom. This pursuit of Zen has helped me immeasurably, improving not only my experience as a teacher, but by giving my entire life a sense of focus, simplicity, and tranquility. It's not an exaggeration to say that, without it, I may not have made it to the end of my career.

I consider myself a peace and self-care artist and an advocate for teacher well-being. I believe in helping teachers create a classroom environment where they don't merely function, but thrive. I believe in helping teachers grow, learn, and, perhaps, most importantly, find joy in their chosen calling. I decided to become an advocate for teacher well-being when I realized that, if teachers are receiving any care at all in the current educational climate, it is coming from themselves and each other.

This is the spirit with which I wrote *The Zen Teacher*. I wrote it with the sincere intention that the ideas, concepts, and exercises will help you find your own sense of peace in the classroom—so you can continue and thrive on your path.

In closing, I'd like to invite you to communicate with me about the things in this book that have worked for you. And those that haven't. In fact, I would love to hear from you about any area of teaching. Feel free to send me a note via the contact form at my website at TheZenTeacher.com, send me an email at teachingzen@gmail.com, or tweet me @thezenteacher. Please also feel free to contact me about giving a Zen Teacher workshop or speaking at your school district, individual site, or other professional development event.

I know that these concepts and practices aren't easy to implement. I'm still struggling with them myself. But that's what teaching and learning is—reaching out in the dark, trying, stumbling, and sometimes flat-out failing until we get our minds around a certain thought. Then the light finally goes on, we ultimately grow, and a little *satori* becomes a reality.

Like learning, becoming a Zen Teacher isn't a process that you will ever finish. It's an ongoing path that's well worth traveling.

So be kind to yourself.

Don't judge.

And be generous with the radical self-care.

I said earlier, Zen (like teaching) is not about the destination, but the journey. And not only have I found a new way to love the journey during the past two decades, but I want to tell you right here and now how glad I am that you're traveling with me.

Peace,
Danny

Bibliography

Austin, Miriam, *Meditation for Wimps* (New York: Sterling, 2003).

Babatua, Leo, "About., *Zen Habits Blog*. Accessed August 30, 2015, http://zenhabits.net/about/.

Babatua, Leo, "Why Living a Life of Gratitude Can Make You Happy," *Zen Habits Blog*, September 13, 2007. Accessed August 30, 2015, http://zenhabits.net/why-living-a-life-of-gratitude-can-make-you-happy/.

Battaglia, Andy, "David Lynch," *A. V. Club*, January 23, 2007. Accessed August 30, 2015. http://www.avclub.com/article/david-lynch-14054.

Burgess, Dave, *Teach Like a Pirate: Increase Student Engagement, Boost Your Creativity and Transform Your Life as an Educator* (San Diego: Dave Burgess Consulting, 2012).

Campbell, Joseph, *The Power of Myth* (New York: Doubleday, 1988).

Chopra, Deepak, *Seven Spiritual Laws for Success: A Practical Guide to the Fulfillment of Your Dreams* (Novato, CA: New World Library, 1994).

Csikszentmihalyi, Mihaly, *Flow: The Psychology of Optimal Experience* (New York: Harper & Row, 1990).

Dalai Lama, *The Art of Happiness: A Handbook for Living* (New York: Riverhead Books, 1998).

Dass, Ram, *Be Here Now*. (San Cristobal, NM: Lama Foundation, 1971).

Davis, Martha, Elizabeth Robbins Eshelman, and Matthew McKay, *The Relaxation & Stress Reduction Handbook* (Oakland, CA: New Harbinger Publications, Inc., 2008).

Dylan, Bob. *Watching the River Flow*. New York: Columbia Records, 1971. http://www.bobdylan.com/us/songs/watching-river-flow.

Gallo, Carmine. "Steve Jobs: Get Rid of the Crappy Stuff." *Forbes*, May 16, 2011. Accessed August 30, 2015. http://www.forbes.com/sites/carminegallo/2011/05/16/steve-jobs-get-rid-of-the-crappy-stuff/.

Goldberg, Natalie. *Writing Down the Bones: Freeing the Writer Within.* Boston: Shambhala Classics, 2005.

Halifax, Joan, "Joan Halifax Roshi: The Abbot at Upaya," *The Upaya Zen Center*. Accessed August 30, 2015. https://www.upaya.org/about/roshi/.

Herrigel, Eugene, *Zen in the Art of Archery* (New York: Pantheon Books, 1953).

Joel, Billy, *The Stranger* (New York: Columbia Records, 1977).

Kabat-Zinn, Jon, *Wherever You Go, There You Are: Mindfulness Meditation in Everyday Life* (New York: Hyperion, 1994).

Kafka, Franz, *The Zürau Aphorisms,* Translated by Michael Hoffman (New York: Schocken Books, 2006).

Kleon, Austin, *Steal Like an Artist: 10 Things Nobody Told You About Being Creative.* (New York: Workman Publishing Company, Inc., 2012).

Kornfield, Jack, "Heaven & Hell," *The Jack Kornfield Blog*. October 6, 2014. Accessed August 30, 2015. http://www.jackkornfield.com/heaven-hell/.

Kreider, Tim, "The Busy Trap," *The New York Times*, June 30 2012. Accessed August 30, 2015. http://opinionator.blogs.nytimes.com/2012/06/30/the-busy-trap/?_r=0.

Kuckinskas, Susan, "Meditation Heals Body and Mind," *WebMD*. Accessed August 30, 2015. http://www.webmd.com/mental-health/features/meditation-heals-body-and-mind.

Lamott, Anne, "Becoming the Person You Were Meant to Be: Where to Start," *O, The Oprah Magazine*, November 2009. Accessed August 30, 2015. http://www.oprah.com/spirit/How-To-Find-Out-Who-You-Really-Are-by-Anne-Lamott.

Lao Tzu, *Tao Te Ching*, Edited by Stephen Mitchell (Harper Perennial, 2009).

Lorde, Audre, *A Burst of Light: Essays by Audre Lorde* (Ithaca, NY: Firebrand Books, 1988).

Office of Naval Research. *More than a Feeling: ONR Investigates 'Spidey Sense' for Sailors and Marines.* (Arlington, VA, 2014).

Penn, William, *Advice of William Penn to His Children: Relating to Their Civil and Religious Conduct* (Philadelphia, Franklin Roberts: 1881).

Ryan Hyde, Catherine, *The Long, Steep Path: Everyday Inspiration from the Author of Pay It Forward.* (Amazon Digital Services, Inc., 2014).

Salk, Jonas, *Anatomy of Reality: Merging of Intuition and Reason* (New York: Columbia UP, 1983).

Salzberg, Shannon, *Lovingkindness: The Revolutionary Art of Happiness* (Boston: Shambhala Classics, 1995).

Suzuki, Shunryu, *Zen Mind, Beginner's Mind* (New York: Weatherhill, 1970).

Tolle, Eckhart, *The Power of Now* (Novato, CA: New World Library, 1999).

Wang, Shirley S., "Coffee Break? Walk in the Park? Why Unwinding Is Hard," *The Wall Street Journal*, August 30, 2011. Accessed September 2, 2015. http://on.wsj.com/ovahFk

Watts, Alan W., *The Way of Zen,* (New York: Pantheon Books, 1957).

Also from

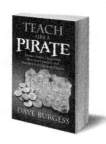

DAVE **B**URGESS
Consulting, Inc.

TEACH LIKE A PIRATE

Increase Student Engagement, Boost Your Creativity, and Transform Your Life as an Educator
By Dave Burgess (@BurgessDave)

Teach Like a PIRATE is the *New York Times'* best-selling book that has sparked a worldwide educational revolution. It is part inspirational manifesto that ignites passion for the profession, and part practical road map filled with dynamic strategies to dramatically increase student engagement. Translated into multiple languages, its message resonates with educators who want to design outrageously creative lessons and transform school into a life-changing experience for students.

P IS FOR PIRATE

Inspirational ABC's for Educators
By Dave and Shelley Burgess (@Burgess_Shelley)

Teaching is an adventure that stretches the imagination and calls for creativity every day! In *P is for Pirate*, husband and wife team, Dave and Shelley Burgess, encourage and inspire educators to make their classrooms fun and exciting places to learn. Tapping into years of personal experience and drawing on the insights of more than seventy educators, the authors offer a wealth of ideas for making learning and teaching more fulfilling than ever before.

PURE GENIUS
Building a Culture of Innovation and Taking 20% Time to the Next Level
By Don Wettrick (@DonWettrick)

For far too long, schools have been bastions of boredom, killers of creativity, and way too comfortable with compliance and conformity. In *Pure Genius,* Don Wettrick explains how collaboration—with experts, students, and other educators—can help you create interesting, and even life-changing, opportunities for learning. Wettrick's book inspires and equips educators with a systematic blueprint for teaching innovation in any school.

LEARN LIKE A PIRATE
Empower Your Students to Collaborate, Lead, and Succeed
By Paul Solarz (@PaulSolarz)

Today's job market demands that students be prepared to take responsibility for their lives and careers. We do them a disservice if we teach them how to earn passing grades without equipping them to take charge of their education. In *Learn Like a Pirate*, Paul Solarz explains how to design classroom experiences that encourage students to take risks and explore their passions in a stimulating, motivating, and supportive environment where improvement, rather than grades, is the focus. Discover how student-led classrooms help students thrive and develop into self-directed, confident citizens who are capable of making smart, responsible decisions, all on their own.

DITCH THAT TEXTBOOK
Free Your Teaching and Revolutionize
Your Classroom
By Matt Miller (@jmattmiller)

Textbooks are symbols of centuries of old education. They're often outdated as soon as they hit students' desks. Acting "by the textbook" implies compliance and a lack of creativity. It's time to ditch those textbooks—and those textbook assumptions about learning! In *Ditch That Textbook*, teacher and blogger Matt Miller encourages educators to throw out meaningless, pedestrian teaching and learning practices. He empowers them to evolve and improve on old, standard, teaching methods. *Ditch That Textbook* is a support system, toolbox, and manifesto to help educators free their teaching and revolutionize their classrooms.

50 THINGS YOU CAN DO WITH GOOGLE CLASSROOM
By Alice Keeler and Libbi Miller

It can be challenging to add new technology to the classroom but it's a must if students are going to be well-equipped for the future. Alice Keeler and Libbi Miller shorten the learning curve by providing a thorough overview of the Google Classroom App. Part of Google Apps for Education (GAfE), Google Classroom was specifically designed to help teachers save time by streamlining the process of going digital. Complete with screenshots, *50 Things You Can Do with Google Classroom* provides ideas and step-by-step instructions to help teachers implement this powerful tool.

MASTER THE MEDIA
How Teaching Media Literacy Can Save Our
Plugged-in World
By Julie Smith

Written to help teachers and parents educate the next generation, *Master the Media* explains the history, purpose, and messages behind the media. The point isn't to get kids to unplug; it's to help them make informed choices, understand the difference between truth and lies, and discern perception from reality. Critical thinking leads to smarter decisions—and it's why media literacy can save the world.

Acknowledgments

Much like teaching, writing starts as a solitary act but ends as a collaborative one. So I'd like to express my gratitude to those who helped make this book possible. My deep and heartfelt thanks go to:

Dave and Shelley Burgess for their excellent support, encouragement, and belief in this book, as well as for being such all-around great people.

Genesis Kohler for creating such a lovely book cover and editor Erin K. Casey and her team at My Writers' Connection for giving my manuscript its own version of "flow." You are truly artists.

Erika Thornes, for the photographic skill and artistic excellence she delivered in the author headshot.

My parents, Michael and Janet Tricarico, who believed unconditionally in every single dream I ever had.

Valerie, Tatum, and Tessa, for their love, support, laughter, and patience. You are the Zen Masters of my life.

The West Hills High School English department, especially Jane Schaffer, Anne Foster, and John Holler, three mentors who saw a scattered and inexperienced drama major and former actor and turned him into an English teacher.

Chris Morrissey, my all-time favorite teacher and an excellent model of skillful teaching, consistent character, and personal integrity. No one gets to where I am without a teacher like Mr. Morrissey somewhere in the backstory.

I would also like to thank the following people, whose unique contributions have improved the quality of my teaching, my writing, my spirituality, and/or my life: Kim Cruise, Ed Hollingsworth, Judith Patterson, Marge Curry, Lucinda Holshue, Terry Theroux, Paula Skrifvars, Geoffrey Anderson, Suzanne Akemi Sannwald, Ed Rintye, the Lackey family, Pablo, Donald Shimoda, Suzanne Geba, Judy Hill Gagne, Lara Zielin, Heather Ophir, Laura Preble, Jeff and DeAnna Thill, Robin LemMon, David Stanley, and Teresa Shea.

More than teachers.

More than friends.

About the Author

Dan Tricarico is a high school English teacher and author of *You're a Teacher . . . So Act Like One! Improving Your Stage Presence in the Classroom.* In his spare time, he enjoys reading and writing, listening to classic rock, staring out of windows, and watching old sitcoms. Dan shares the Zen Teacher experience around the country as a presenter and speaker.

CPSIA information can be obtained at www.ICGtesting.com
Printed in the USA
BVOW06s2144161115

427409BV00019B/146/P